FAITH

JOY

and

HOPE

Publications International, Ltd.

Louis Weber, CEO
Publications International, Ltd.
8140 Lehigh Avenue
Morton Grove, IL 60053

Permission is never granted for commercial purposes.

ISBN: 978-1-63938-662-8

Manufactured in China.

8 7 6 5 4 3 2 1

Let's get social!

 @Publications_International

@PublicationsInternational

www.pilbooks.com

Table of Contents

Introduction

Your relationship with the Lord is constantly evolving and continually pro-
viding hope and joy even in dark times.
Taking time each day to reflect and converse with God is the best way to grow
in your faith. *Faith, Joy, and Hope* is a
tool to do just that. Use this book as a
guide to your reflections and grow closer
to the Lord.

This book includes nine chapters, with
each chapter dealing with the continual
journey of faith and seeking joy in your
personal relationship with God. Each
chapter contains a variety of prayers,
scripture verses, inspirational quotes,

and hymns addressing situations, burdens, and jubilations you may experience in your own life.

To use this book, set aside some time and find a quiet, restful place where you can sit in stillness with the Lord. Choose a chapter that resonates with you and reflect on prayers that speak to your situation. Let the words on the page guide you into forming your own thoughts and contemplating what it means to live in God's light.

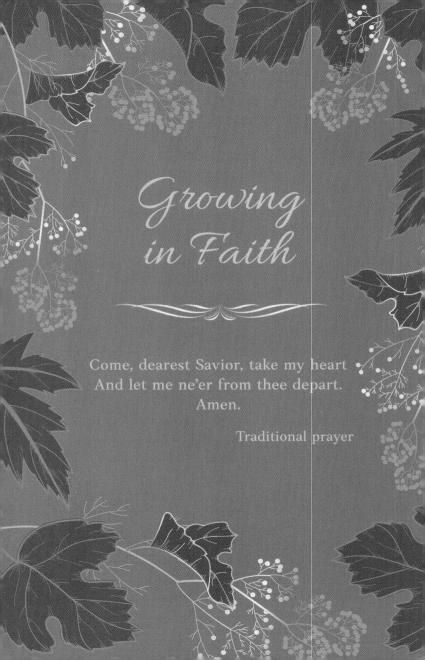

Growing
in Faith

Come, dearest Savior, take my heart
And let me ne'er from thee depart.
Amen.

Traditional prayer

Faithful Shepherd, feed me
In the pastures green;
Faithful Shepherd, lead me
Where thy steps are seen.
Hold me fast and guide me
In the narrow way;
So, with thee beside me,
I shall never stray.
Daily bring me nearer
To the heavenly shore;
May my faith grow clearer.
May I love thee more!
Hallow every pleasure,
Every gift and pain;
Be thyself my treasure.
Though none else I gain.

—Thomas Benson Pollock

O God, who hast folded back the mantle of the night to clothe us in the golden glory of the day, chase from our hearts all gloomy thoughts, and make us glad with the brightness of hope, that we may effectively aspire to unwon virtues, through Jesus Christ our Lord. Amen.

6th-century prayer

Hast thou not known? hast thou not heard, that the everlasting God, the Lord, the Creator of the ends of the earth, fainteth not, neither is weary? there is no searching of his understanding.

Isaiah 40:28

God never gets tired of you, even when you fail or falter over and over again. He is your everlasting God and creator. He always understands and never faints, not just in his care for you, but for his people from one end of the earth to the other. How great and majestic and wise he is. You can relax. He will always be there to help.

Serena and her husband Jim moved to their new home during winter, and she'd looked forward to the neighborhood's annual summer block party. She figured she'd meet new people; what she didn't anticipate was that her faith might be challenged. "So you're one of those religious types?" a woman laughed, upon learning that Serena and Jim attended a church nearby. Though uncomfortable, Serena dug deep: "Yes," she responded with polite firmness. "We've found happiness in our new church home." Dear Lord, sometimes I am asked to justify my faith; sometimes I am even mocked for it. Please strengthen my heart and give me the right words and spirit to articulate my belief.

*Take heed therefore unto yourselves,
and to all the flock, over which the
Holy Ghost hath made you overseers,
to feed the church of God, which he
hath purchased with his own blood.*

Acts 20:28

Lord, I thank you today for the full
community of believers. We are not alone
in seeking you out, and in worshiping you.
Being around other people of faith can renew
my own. I pray today for all that call out to
you. May our faith flourish.

Then Ahimelech answered the king, and said, And who is so faithful among all thy servants as David, which is the king's son in law, and goeth at thy bidding, and is honorable in thine house?

1 Samuel 22:14

I have traditionally thought of faith as a way to keep strong my personal connection to God. But this week I found myself in conversation with a new workmate, an atheist, who asked me point blank whether I believe in God. When I avowed that I do, my companion asked what sustains that conviction, to which I replied simply, "Faith." That night, as I reviewed the conversation, I felt relief that I had made my beliefs clear. To downplay them, I realized, would have felt like a betrayal. In that moment I was struck by the revolutionary idea that God wants us to be faithful simply to . . . serve him. Dear Lord, help me to remember that faith is more than a means of strengthening my relationship with you—it's also a way of serving you.

My imagination creates a vision of what I want in my life. God then points me to the resources, people, and things I need to make that vision come alive. My only job is to have faith that all is unfolding according to his divine plans.

Father, I abandon myself into your hands; do with me what you will.

Whatever you may do, I thank you: I am ready for all, I accept all.

Let only your will be done in me, and in all your creatures—

I wish no more than this, O Lord.

—Charles de Foucauld

And when the children of Israel saw it, they said one to another, It is manna: for they wist not what it was. And Moses said unto them, This is the bread which the Lord hath given you to eat.

Exodus 16:15

Father, please instill in me a desire to seek out and delight in your holy Word. Please give me insight when I read the scriptures, that your words illuminate my life, even when the truth is hard to hear because it demands something from me that I don't want to give.

Who guides and protects me in my life? Today, I am grateful for the people who have brought me to where I am today and who always have my best interests at heart. I may not always have appreciated their guidance, but I know deep down they always meant well. In the same way, Lord, let me accept and appreciate your guidance in my life.

*And as Moses lifted up the serpent
in the wilderness, even so must
the Son of man be lifted up: That
whosoever believeth in him should
not perish, but have eternal life.*

John 3:14–15

The Israelites had sinned and were being
judged. People lay sick in their tents, and
many died. Then God commanded Moses
to do a strange thing. He put a pole in the
center of the camp with a bronze snake on
it. All people had to do was look at it to be
cured. Jesus tells us that he too would be
lifted up. And all we have to do is look and
believe. It doesn't seem like much. But it is
more than enough.

I wish to be of service, Lord.
So give me courage to
put my own hope and despair,
my own doubt and fear
at the disposal of others.
For how could I ever help without
first being, simply . . . real?

Beth, an attorney, is invited to constantly debate on behalf of what she believes is right. Every day she goes into work, she deals with conflict, and her "opponents" are articulate people with well-crafted arguments. It can be draining and emotionally taxing, but she is inspired by God's exhortation to speak out. Dear Lord, Corinthians tells me that you were there for people in biblical times when they had to debate. I believe that you are there for me, too, every day, when I am challenged to speak out.

Casting down imaginations, and every high thing that exalteth itself against the knowledge of God, and bringing into captivity every thought to the obedience of Christ.

2 Corinthians 10:5

Lord, how it must amuse you at times to see us orchestrating the details of our days as if everything and everyone were in our control. It's only when you are involved in our plans that things go smoothly, Lord. Teach us to trust that your way is the better way, even when we can't see how every detail will turn out. Our insight is only as good as our reliance on you. Please be with us each day, Lord.

But we are not of them who draw back unto perdition; but of them that believe to the saving of the soul.

Hebrews 10:39

My daughter has a child's Bible, and she loves the stories about Jesus and the miracles he wrought: water into wine, healing the sick. "Dad, why don't we see miracles like this anymore?" she asked me just yesterday. Her question echoed a wish I have had on more than one occasion: living in a society so bent on flash, on the next best thing, I myself have yearned to see visible signs of God's presence. But as my daughter and I talked, we began to acknowledge the presence of miracles in the everyday: the antibiotic she took last week for an ear infection; the rosemary seeds we'd planted together, which are gaining traction and sprouting up. Health and new life burgeon behind the scenes: our world is, in fact, full of miracles! And when we cannot recognize them for the miracles they are? Then we must rely on faith. God, help me to see the miracles in my life, and strengthen me to have faith even when I don't see visible signs of your presence.

But by the grace of God I am what I am: and his grace which was bestowed upon me was not in vain; but I labored more abundantly than they all: yet not I, but the grace of God which was with me.

1 Corinthians 15:10

Sometimes I take pride in my faith. I favorably compare my church involvement to that of others; I share a helpful spiritual practice with a friend not with humility but with an air of condescension. Lord, keep me gentle and humble of heart, aware of how reliant I am on you.

God, I hear your call to action, and I am ready to do your mighty will in all areas of my life, and in the world. Guide and direct my path as I step out in faith.

Teach me to do thy will; for thou art my God: thy spirit is good; lead me into the land of uprightness.

Psalm 143:10

O God, all the instruction and guidance we need to live a purposeful life is provided for us in your Word. So why do we find ourselves allured by commentators on talk shows or by self-help gurus with all the latest and purportedly greatest approaches to life's problems? Keep me in your perfect will for my life, God, and prevent me from being pulled this way and that by all the influences this world promotes. For I know that it is only when you are leading me that I am moving in the right direction.

I trust, O Lord, your holy name;
O let me not be put to shame
nor let me be confounded.
My faith, O Lord,
be in your Word
forever firmly grounded.

—Adam Reissner,
trans. Catherine Winkworth

As for me, I will call upon God;
and the Lord shall save me.

Psalm 55:16

Your grandma's prayers won't save you. They may help you. Only heaven knows the good in the world done by generations of faithful, praying people. If you want the Lord to save you, though, you have to call on him yourself. This requires your recognition of your need and his mercy. The Psalmist continues in the next verse: "Evening, and morning, and at noon, will I pray, and cry aloud: and he shall hear my voice." That is prayer that saves.

Lord,
My faith in you fortifies me, and gives me strength. My faith in you is like nourishment when I am hungry or water when I am thirsty. It gives me life and energy and hope. My faith in you overcomes all fears, doubts and insecurities, knowing that it isn't me doing the work, but you working through me. My faith in you is life-sustaining and creates miracles big and small everywhere I go. The results of my faith in you, Lord, are the abundant blessings you shower upon me for simply believing and trusting in you. Amen.

But the scripture hath concluded all under sin, that the promise by faith of Jesus Christ might be given to them that believe.

Galatians 3:22

Faith is more than a passive idea; it is a principle of action that motivates our day-to-day decisions and actions. Would a farmer plant if he did not expect to harvest? Would the student read and study if she did not believe it would improve the quality of her life? Would we work hard each day if we did not hope that by doing so we might accomplish something worthwhile?

We daily act upon things we believe in, though we cannot yet see the end result. This is the faith we live by, whether we identify it as such or not.

As faithful people, we take this principle one step further: We do things that are motivated by our faith in things promised but not yet fulfilled. We smile in the face of adversity. We continue in prayer even when our prayers don't seem to be answered. We stop saying, "I can't" and start believing God can! Step by step, we put our faith into action and learn to "live by faith."

*Heaven and earth shall pass away:
but my words shall not pass away.*

Luke 21:33

Each day, this book of promises and prayers
points you to the words of God. Ponder this:
Each verse you read will never pass away,
even if heaven fails and the earth dissolves.
Nothing is more permanent than God's
promises. Nothing is more stable than his
Scripture. Nothing is worth more than his
Word. Treasure it. Store it in your heart.
Delight in it. Meditate on it. Believe it. It
shall not pass away.

Jesus had promised his followers that he would die, then rise again. Sometimes he spoke in parables, though, and perhaps they thought (or hoped) he was speaking metaphorically. But then on that morning—that mind-blowing morning—when Jesus exited his tomb in triumph over our nemesis death, there was no doubt that he had meant what he had said. "Look!" the angel exclaimed. In other words, "See for yourself that it's true." Jesus has risen, and he opened the way to eternal life for all who trust in him.

The Lord will give strength unto his people; the Lord will bless his people with peace.

Psalm 29:11

God strengthens individuals, but he also strengthens groups. This thought gave me comfort last night as I prepared for a summer mission trip. I will be traveling to Oklahoma to help rebuild homes destroyed in a tornado, and have been charged with directing eight college-aged kids from my church. I am a skilled carpenter but less certain about leading a group. God, I pray you will grant my team the strength and cohesiveness we need to do our jobs well.

Most gracious God, to know and love whose will is righteousness, enlighten our souls with the brightness of thy presence, that we may both know thy will and be enabled to perform it; through Jesus Christ our Lord. Amen.

11th-century prayer

Blessed are they which are persecuted for righteousness' sake: for theirs is the kingdom of heaven.

Matthew 5:10

Lord, I get frustrated sometimes, when others are not acting rightly. But you never promised an easy road for those who believe in you. Let me be gentle but persistent in carrying your truth to the world, and not wither in the face of scorn.

I come to the garden alone while
the dew is still on the roses

And the voice I hear falling on
my ear the Son of God discloses

And he walks with me,
and he talks with me

And he tells me I am his own

And the joy we share
as we tarry there

None other has ever known.

—C. Austin Miles

These all died in faith, not having received the promises, but having seen them afar off, and were persuaded of them, and embraced them, and confessed that they were strangers and pilgrims on the earth.

Hebrews 11:13

God's promises are true, but we don't always live to see them fulfilled. You can still believe them, embrace them, and be comforted by them, however. That's because this is not our final destination. We are just passing through, on our way to a better homeland where all will be fulfilled and revealed. Enjoy the journey, knowing that it's not the destination.

Some days the race feels like a sprint, Lord, and on other days, a marathon. I want to press on, but I need you to infuse my spirit with your strength and steadfastness. I want to run and finish well. Thank you for beginning the work of faith in my life and for promising not to stop working until my faith is complete.

Lord,
I am having trouble forgiving someone who betrayed me. I know that it would be what you want, but don't have the strength to let it go. Please help me look deep within to find that strength and to allow myself and this other person the gift of forgiveness. You have always forgiven me my mistakes and shortcomings, help me to do the same for someone else and release us both from the bondage of anger and disappointment. Amen.

And when ye stand praying, forgive, if ye have ought against any: that your Father also which is in heaven may forgive you your trespasses.

Mark 11:25

Dear Lord,
Hear my prayer. I thank you for never losing faith in me, and for never giving up on me. My problem is, so often the ways of the world cause me to lose faith in my fellow men and women, and in myself. I pray for a stronger faith in all of your beloved children, even those that don't behave in ways I approve of. I pray for the kind of trust in life that sees beyond surface appearances and judgments. I pray today, dear Lord, for a deeper bond with you so that no matter what goes on in the world, I am at peace. Amen.

For whatsoever is born of God overcometh the world: and this is the victory that overcometh the world, even our faith.

1 John 5:4

I have set the Lord always before me: because he is at my right hand, I shall not be moved.

Psalm 16:8

The right hand is a place of honor and, for most, a place of strength. So God is honored when our awareness and knowledge of him is always before us. When we wake up in the middle of the night and when we deal with difficult people at work, he is close at hand. Because he is, we will not be moved or rattled. Set him before you this moment. And in all the moments of your day.

Lord,
I know that I am only human, and not meant to understand your mysterious ways. To me, life sometimes makes no sense, and things happen I just can't wrap my mind around. Please help me have a sense of peace, a sense of understanding that it all does make sense, and that everything happens for a reason, even if you are the only one who knows what that reason is. Help me feel more balance, harmony, and serenity even when I'm afraid and uncertain. Your love alone can make me feel as though everything is just the way it was meant to be, and that my life does have purpose and meaning. Thank you, Lord. Amen.

*Give me understanding,
and I shall keep thy law; yea, I shall
observe it with my whole heart.*

Psalm 119:34

Faith and fear cannot coexist. One always gives way to the other. It is necessary for us to be constantly building up our faith to overcome the numerous sources of destructive disbelief all around us. We need to be continually working at rekindling the gift of God that is in us, which is our faith in him and in his promises. We must be dedicated to developing a spirit of love and power and discipline within ourselves. Studying the words of the scriptures, meditating on them, keeping God's commandments, and praying daily are some of the ways we can keep our faith strong. By focusing on these things, we shut out fear and cultivate faith.

And being not weak in faith, he considered not his own body now dead, when he was about an hundred years old, neither yet the deadness of Sarah's womb: He staggered not at the promise of God through unbelief; but was strong in faith, giving glory to God; And being fully persuaded that, what he had promised, he was able also to perform.

Romans 4:19–21

The Bible makes much of Abraham's faith, which is remarkable and instructive. God had promised him a son, and even though he and his wife were both in their late 90s, Abraham believed God could and would keep his promise. He staggered not at the promise of God. God's promise to us is surely as remarkable, salvation by grace through the atoning work of God's own Son. Our response should be the same: Be strong in faith, giving glory to God.

We beseech thee, O Lord, let our hearts be graciously enlightened by thy holy radiance, that we may serve thee without fear in holiness and righteousness all the days of our life; that so we may escape the darkness of this world, and by thy guidance attain the land of eternal brightness; through thy mercy, O blessed Lord, who dost live and govern all things, world without end. Amen.

11th-century prayer

That we should be to the praise of his glory, who first trusted in Christ. In whom ye also trusted, after that ye heard the word of truth, the gospel of your salvation: in whom also after that ye believed, ye were sealed with that holy Spirit of promise, Which is the earnest of our inheritance until the redemption of the purchased possession, unto the praise of his glory.

Ephesians 1:12–14

The great promise here is that those who have trusted Christ are sealed with the Holy Spirit. It is like the earnest money God pays to secure an investment. It is the proof that you will receive the inheritance he promised. As the Spirit of God reminds you of God's Word and promises, his presence reminds you that it is all true. This all results, as it should, in the praise of his glory.

*Blessed is the man that walketh not
in the counsel of the ungodly, nor
standeth in the way of sinners, nor
sitteth in the seat of the scornful.
But his delight is in the law of the
Lord; and in his law doth he meditate
day and night.
And he shall be like a tree planted by
the rivers of water, that bringeth forth
his fruit in his season; his leaf also
shall not wither; and whatsoever he
doeth shall prosper.
The ungodly are not so:
but are like the chaff which
the wind driveth away.
Therefore the ungodly shall not stand
in the judgment, nor sinners in the
congregation of the righteous.
For the Lord knoweth the way of the
righteous: but the way of the ungodly
shall perish.*

Psalm 1

Blessed are the peacemakers: for they shall be called the children of God.

Matthew 5:9

What does it mean to be a peacemaker? Not to overlook wrongs, or to speak soothing platitudes, but to work out conflicts by listening to God's will. Bless those who do the work of restoring relationships in accordance with God's plan.

The central issue
of the Bible is
whether we live it.

—John Alexander

The Hope Within

Without Christ there is no hope.

Charles Spurgeon

Fear thou not; for I am with thee: be not dismayed; for I am thy God: I will strengthen thee; yea, I will help thee; yea, I will uphold thee with the right hand of my righteousness.

Isaiah 41:10

Knowing and obeying God's Word gives us life, but not only in the sense of knowing how to live. It gives us actual life. In John 3, when speaking to Nicodemus, Jesus referred to this as being "born again," alive to new possibilities and new potential. This new reality is a spiritual one, with new insights and new power, drawn from the very Spirit of God. And we don't even have to live this life by ourselves; he upholds us, keeping and strengthening us according to his Word.

Hope, like the glimmering taper's light,
Adorns and cheers our way;
And still, as darker grows the night,
Emits a brighter ray.

—Oliver Goldsmith

But they that wait upon the Lord shall renew their strength; they shall mount up with wings as eagles; they shall run, and not be weary; and they shall walk, and not faint.

Isaiah 40:31

I know thy works: behold, I have set before thee an open door, and no man can shut it: for thou hast a little strength, and hast kept my word, and hast not denied my name.

Revelation 3:8

All of the churches to which Jesus (through John) sends letters are under persecution. Not all of them are faithful. But his promises to the faithful are varied and precious. To the church at Philadelphia he promises opportunity and strength. He will protect them and he will come quickly—promises every believer finds comforting and encouraging (verses 7–12). And to the one who overcomes he says he will "write upon him the name of my God, and the name of the city of my God" (verse 12). Even enemies will "know that I have loved thee" (verse 9). To be owned by him and to be known by him is our great desire. It is his great promise for those who have "kept my word."

And not only so, but we glory in tribulations also: knowing that tribulation worketh patience. And patience, experience; and experience, hope. And hope maketh not ashamed; because the love of God is shed abroad in our hearts by the Holy Ghost which is given unto us.

Romans 5:3–5

We are surprised by joy, God of re-creation, when we see despair outwitted by simple acts of love as small as grains of sand. Keep us searching, believing, and building upon them, realizing that grains of sand make dune, shore, and desert.

But rather seek ye the kingdom of God; and all these things shall be added unto you.

Luke 12:31

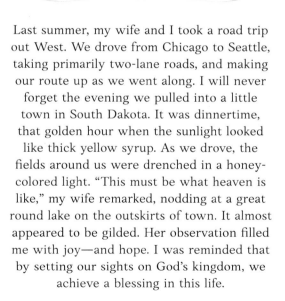

Last summer, my wife and I took a road trip out West. We drove from Chicago to Seattle, taking primarily two-lane roads, and making our route up as we went along. I will never forget the evening we pulled into a little town in South Dakota. It was dinnertime, that golden hour when the sunlight looked like thick yellow syrup. As we drove, the fields around us were drenched in a honey-colored light. "This must be what heaven is like," my wife remarked, nodding at a great round lake on the outskirts of town. It almost appeared to be gilded. Her observation filled me with joy—and hope. I was reminded that by setting our sights on God's kingdom, we achieve a blessing in this life.

The past, O God of yesterdays, todays, and promise-filled tomorrows, can be an anchor or a launching pad. It's sometimes so easy to look back on the pain and hurt and believe the future may be an instant replay. Help us to accept the aches of the past and put them in perspective so we can also see the many ways you supported and nurtured us. Then, believing in your promise of regeneration, launch us into the future free and excited to live in joy.

In this day of bigger is best, Lord, we wonder what difference our little lights can make. Remind us of the laser, so tiny, yet when focused, has infinite power. This little light of mine, O Lord, gives it such focus.

I am the door: by me if any man enter in, he shall be saved, and shall go in and out, and find pasture.

John 10:9

Jesus doesn't say he is like a door. He says he is the door. By faith, all we have to do is open it and walk through. That's how we are saved. And that's how we go in and out, finding a meadow for spiritual rest and a pasture for spiritual food. It seems too simple, but simple is not the same thing as easy. What we want is to find our own way, and it turns out that is not easy at all. It is good to remind ourselves: We only need to walk through the door and be saved. It's that simple.

Left alone now, we drift aimlessly like untied balloons let loose to fly helter-skelter. Yet life goes on and decisions must be made. O God, help us make up minds that won't stay still. Give us good sense to put off until tomorrow what we shouldn't try today. Reassure us this is only temporary, a brief hesitation, not a giving up; hold up a mirror for us to see a once-again clear-eyed person.

God moves in a mysterious way
His wonders to perform
He plants his footsteps in the sea
And rides upon the storm.
Deep in unfathomable mines
Of never-failing skill
He treasures up his bright designs,
And works his sovereign will.
Ye fearful saints fresh courage take;
The clouds ye so much dread
Are big with mercy, and shall break
In blessings on your head.

—William Cowper,
"Light Shining out of Darkness"

Touch and calm my turbulent emotions, God of the still waters. Whisper words to the listening ears of my soul. In hearing your voice, give me assurance beyond a shadow of a doubt that you are my companion in life, eternally.

And Ruth said, Intreat me not to leave thee, or to return from following after thee: for whither thou goest, I will go; and where thou lodgest, I will lodge: thy people shall be my people, and thy God my God.

Ruth 1:16

When Ruth promised to go with Naomi anywhere she went, they were both childless widows, refugees on the road to Bethlehem. Their circumstances were dire, and their prospects were dim. Soon Ruth would be picking up barley left in a field to keep them alive. But they were not only returning to Naomi's people, but to Naomi's God. He would meet their needs and secure their future. This is where their hope, and our hope, begins.

*For the seed shall be prosperous;
the vine shall give her fruit, and the
ground shall give her increase, and
the heavens shall give their dew;
and I will cause the remnant of this
people to possess all these things.*

Zechariah 8:12

Enliven my imagination, God of new life, so that I can see through today's troubles to coming newness. Surround me with your caring so that I can live as if the new has already begun.

The Lord preserveth all them that love him: but all the wicked will he destroy.

Psalm 145:20

We are preserved. And our sovereign Lord will manage the details. We need not keep track of our slights or hold on to our grievances; we can sleep at night because he is just and good. He promises to preserve and protect us. Sometimes he preserves us from others, sometimes from ourselves. But we have no need to worry or fear or plot revenge. We just have to love him more because he preserves those who love him.

Sing the wondrous love of Jesus,
Sing his mercy and his grace;
In the mansions bright and blessed,
He'll prepare for us a place.
While we walk the pilgrim pathway,
Clouds will overspread the sky;
But when trav'ling days are over,
Not a shadow, not a sigh.
When we all get to heaven,
What a day of rejoicing that will be!
When we all see Jesus,
We'll sing and shout the victory.

—Eliza E. Hewitt,
"When We All Get To Heaven"

For by grace are ye saved through faith; and that not of yourselves: it is the gift of God: Not of works, lest any man should boast.

Ephesians 2:8–9

Father God, you gave a staggering gift through your son, Jesus Christ. How can I express my gratitude for the gift of salvation? Sometimes I need to sit in silence, surrounded by your presence, as I reflect on your love for me.

Though like the wanderer,
The sun gone down,
Darkness be over me,
My rest a stone;
Yet in my dreams I'd be
Nearer, my God, to Thee,
Nearer to Thee!
. . . Then, with my waking thoughts
Bright with Thy praise,
out of my stony griefs,
Bethel I'll raise;
So by my woes to be
Nearer, my God, to Thee,
Nearer to Thee!

—Sarah Flower Adams,
"Nearer to Thee"

But I will hope continually, and will yet praise thee more and more.

Psalm 71:14

My old college friend Tom is an artist. He lives in a city near my home, and occasionally he'll have a gallery showing of his work downtown. I always try to make his shows, and we usually also manage to get together for a meal every month or so. His shows are a perfect time for me to compliment his work. But one evening when we were just meeting for dinner, I mentioned how impressed I am by a series of sculptures he's been making from pressed wood. Even though I had already praised that same work at a recent show, the innovative nature of the work has stayed with me, and I wanted to share that. Tom was uplifted by my comment. It turns out he'd had a frustrating day in the studio and my admiration, coming from out of the blue like that, meant a lot to him. The experience reminded me that praise is not a one-time thing—you never know when another person might be struggling, or how much repeating a kind word can mean. God, may I remember to uplift others even as I praise you, again and again.

I always want to be a dreamer, O God, to feel the stir and the yearning to see my vision become reality. There are those who would say dreamers are free-floaters. When I dream I feel connected to you and to your creation, bound by purpose and a sense of call. Nourish my dreams and my striving to make them real.

For it is written in the law of Moses, thou shalt not muzzle the mouth of the ox that treadeth out the corn. Doth God take care for oxen? Or saith he it altogether for our sakes? For our sakes, no doubt, this is written: that he that ploweth should plow in hope; and that he that thresheth in hope should be partaker of his hope.

1 Corinthians 9:9-10

And I will set up one shepherd over them, and he shall feed them, even my servant David; he shall feed them, and he shall be their shepherd.

Ezekiel 34:23

This is the word of the Lord, through Isaiah. God's people will return from exile. The road will be rough, steep, and unknown. But "he that hath mercy on them will lead them." And there is more. He will guide them by "springs of water," as if his mercy were not enough. The Holy Spirit will "guide you into all truth" (John 16:13). Jesus himself came "To give light to them that sit in darkness and in the shadow of death, to guide our feet into the way of peace" (Luke 1:79). And like David, we will lie down in green pastures by still waters (Psalm 23:1–2). Yes, he will guide us. But he will refresh us too.

I have been apart and I have lost my way . . . And in my hours of darkness when I am not even sure there is a Thou hearing my call, I still call to Thee with all my heart. Hear the cry of my voice, clamoring from this desert, for my soul is parched and my heart can barely stand this longing.

Gnostic Holy Eucharist

And God is able to make all grace abound toward you; that ye, always having all sufficiency in all things, may abound to every good work.

2 Corinthians 9:8

Hope, in the biblical sense, is not just wishing something were true. On the contrary, we "abound in hope" because we are joyfully confident that God keeps his promises. Through the power of the Holy Spirit, we know his promises are true. This knowledge fills us with peace and joy, so lacking in the darkness around us. Where there is darkness and despair, we have, and bring, certainty and light. Our hope is a joyful expectation in the kindness of our God.

Life becomes much easier and more
enjoyable when we know we are never
alone. We always have our Higher Power
to turn to for strength, hope, guidance, and
renewal. God is on the job 24 hours a day,
7 days a week, 365 days a year.

Hope springs eternal in the human breast:
Man never is, but always to be, blest.
The soul, uneasy and confin'd from home
Rests and expatiates in a life to come.

—Alexander Pope

Held up to your light, our broken hearts can become prisms that scatter micro-rainbows on the wall. Our pain is useless as it is, redeeming God, just as a prism is a useless chunk of glass until light passes through it. Remind us that the smallest ray of sun in a shower can create a rainbow. Use our tears as the showers and your love as the sun. Looking up, we see the tiniest arches of hope in the lightening sky.

Sometimes, I think, the things we see
Are shadows of the things to be;
That what we plan we build;
That every hope that hath been crossed,
And every dream we thought was lost,
In heaven shall be fulfilled.

—Phoebe Cary

My soul, wait thou only upon God;
for my expectation is from him.
He only is my rock and my
salvation: he is my defence;
I shall not be moved.

Psalm 62:5–6

An anchor digs into the seabed and prevents the ship from drifting due to wind or current. We have an anchor like that, holding us sure and steadfast. With all the shifting currents and winds in our day, our sure hope is that which anchors us to the unchanging purpose and power of God, keeping our soul from drifting away or crashing into a rocky shore.
Thanks be to God.

*The night is far spent, the
day is at hand: let us therefore cast
off the works of darkness, and
let us put on the armor of light.*

Romans 13:12

I go to prepare a place for you. And if I go and prepare a place for you, I will come again, and receive you unto myself; that where I am, there ye may be also.

John 14:2–3

There is a sense in which John 14, 15, and 16 are one long, glorious promise from Christ to his disciples. I'm leaving, but I'm coming back, he tells them. This is a tender moment. He is clearly thinking of his impending crucifixion. But while we would probably be thinking of ourselves, he is thinking of us.

"Let not your heart be troubled," he says (verse 1). There is a place for you in my Father's house. John Bunyan, the author of *Pilgrim's Progress*, said the promises of Jesus are "words for a man to hang his soul upon." We are not discouraged. There is more and better to come. He will come again. Hallelujah.

By whom also we have access by faith into this grace wherein we stand, and rejoice in hope of the glory of God.

Romans 5:2

Dreams are another form of hope;
and hope is God opening a door.

*And it shall come to pass
afterward, that I will pour out my
spirit upon all flesh; and your sons
and your daughters shall prophesy,
your old men shall dream dreams,
your young men shall see visions.*

Joel 2:28

As the mountains are round about Jerusalem, so the Lord is round about his people from henceforth even for ever.

Psalm 125:2

This is one of the Psalms of Ascent (Psalms 120—134), a collection of hymns the Hebrews sang during the Feast Days. We can imagine Jesus sang these as a young man, traveling to the temple with his parents and even traveling to his death with his disciples.

It is comforting to know the Lord surrounds his people and protects them. And it is comforting to know that Jesus himself found strength in the music of faith. "They that trust in the Lord shall be as mount Zion, which cannot be removed, but abideth forever" (verse 1). And we find comfort too in all the songs of Zion.

*And in the fourth watch of the night Jesus went
unto them, walking on the sea.*

*And when the disciples saw him walking
on the sea, they were troubled, saying, It is
a spirit; and they cried out for fear.*

*But straightway Jesus spake unto them, saying,
Be of good cheer; it is I; be not afraid.*

*And Peter answered him and said, Lord,
if it be thou, bid me come unto thee on the water.*

*And he said, Come. And when Peter
was come down out of the ship, he walked
on the water, to go to Jesus.*

*But when he saw the wind boisterous,
he was afraid; and beginning to sink,
he cried, saying, Lord, save me.*

*And immediately Jesus stretched forth his hand,
and caught him, and said unto him, O thou of little
faith, wherefore didst thou doubt?*

*And when they were come into the ship,
the wind ceased.*

Matthew 14:25–32

Whatever tests in life you're facing, whether it's a challenge of relationships, finances, or your career, the loving Spirit that created you is always available to guide you into a better life.

And whatsoever ye shall ask in my name, that will I do, that the Father may be glorified in the Son. If ye shall ask any thing in my name, I will do it.

John 14:13–14

Wow! If we ask anything he will do it. Is it as simple as just saying "In Jesus' name" at the end of our prayer? Of course not. Because "in His name" is clearly bounded by the Father's glory. That is what Jesus often prayed for.

He pointed to the Father over and over again, saying, "the Father that dwelleth in me, he doeth the works" (verse 10). To pray in Jesus' name, then, is to pray for what the Father wants. He may not want us to have what we want right now. In fact, he may want us to pray for the opportunity to care for others in a way that makes them thank God. Like Jesus, we pray that the Father may be glorified.

For thou hast delivered my soul from death: wilt not thou deliver my feet from falling, that I may walk before God in the light of the living?

Psalm 56:13

Man was made for Joy & Woe;

And when this we rightly know

Thro' the World we safely go,

Joy & Woe are woven fine,

A Clothing for the Soul divine.

—William Blake,
"Auguries of Innocence"

Joyful Hearts

I delight to do thy will,
O my God: yea,
thy law is within my heart.

Psalm 40:8

Let us all with gladsome voice
praise the God of heaven,
who, to bid our hearts rejoice,
his own Son has given.
To this vale of tears he comes,
here to serve in sadness,
that with him in heav'n's fair homes
we may reign in gladness.

—Urban Langhans,
trans. Catherine Winkworth

Jesus, thou joy of loving hearts!
Thou fount of life! Thou light of men!
From the best bliss that earth imparts,
We turn unfilled to thee again.
Thy truth unchanged hath ever stood;
Thou savest those that on thee call;
To them that seek thee, thou art good,
To them that find thee—All in All!

12th-century prayer
attributed to Bernard of Clairvaux

*Therefore will I offer in
his tabernacle sacrifices of joy;
I will sing, yea, I will sing
praises unto the Lord.*

Psalm 27:6

Today I want to praise your name, God.
I want to be joyful in a way that spills
over, full of awe and thanksgiving. I want
to make a sacrifice of praise, to revel in
the works of your hands, to delight in
your awesome power.

And whatsoever ye do in word or deed, do all in the name of the Lord Jesus, giving thanks to God and the Father by him.

Colossians 3:17

Some days are joyful. Yesterday was such a day. I attended church, it was a good sermon, and as the pastor led us in prayer, my thankfulness sprang forth easily. It felt good to thank you, God. When I walked out into the world, it was as though I was smiling and the world smiled back at me. At lunch I swapped jokes with our waitress and thanked her by leaving a good tip. When we stopped by the nursing home where my dad lives, I appreciated the time I was able to spend laughing and talking with some of the residents. One older gentleman who served in World War II relayed a story about his experiences, and I thanked him for sharing. "You are a happy person," he commented. "I can tell by your gratitude." I was deeply touched by his statement, and reminded that showing appreciation to others, not only in words but in actions, is one way of passing on the thankfulness we feel in our own hearts. Dear Lord, help me to always give thanks to you in the way I conduct myself.

The joy of God be in thy face,

Joy to all who see thee,

The circle of God around thy neck,

Angels of God shielding thee,

Angels of God shielding thee.

Joy of night and day be thine,

Joy of sun and moon be thine,

Joy of men and women be thine,

Each land and sea thou goest,

Each land and sea thou goest.

Be every season happy for thee,

Be every season bright for thee,

Be everyone glad for thee.

Thou beloved one of my breast.

Thou beloved one of my heart.

Carla does not consider herself the type of person who proselytizes; she believes actions speak louder than words. But she personally finds the scriptures to be beautiful, particularly the book of Psalms. She's committed some passages to memory, and will sometimes quote them as a way of sharing their beauty. "I guess this is how I express my faith," Carla said. "To me, it's like sharing a poem. I'm communicating something that brings me joy." Dear Lord, please help me to be a teacher in my own way!

All scripture is given by inspiration of God, and is profitable for doctrine, for reproof, for correction, for instruction in righteousness.

2 Timothy 3:16

Bless you, Lord!

The heavens declare your glory;

the skies proclaim your mighty power.

And here I am, looking up into

those vast regions, knowing

that the tiniest cell in my body

is a most glorious miracle, as well.

Bless you, Lord!

Make a joyful noise unto the Lord, all ye lands. Serve the Lord with gladness: come before his presence with singing. Know ye that the Lord he is God: it is he that hath made us, and not we ourselves; we are his people, and the sheep of his pasture. Enter into his gates with thanksgiving, and into his courts with praise: be thankful unto him, and bless his name. For the Lord is good; his mercy is everlasting; and his truth endureth to all generations.

Psalm 100

Today is a good day to praise the Lord. It's a good day to make a list of all his blessings. Begin with life itself and his truth which lasts forever. After that add his provision, which includes any food you like or any beauty you observe. Be concrete and specific. Make the list and then thank him. Thank him in song. Thank him in prayer. Thank him in everyday conversations with a friend or chance encounters with a stranger. Because he is good, and his mercy is everlasting, and he is worthy of our praise.

All praise to Him who now hath turned

My fears to joys, my sighs to song,

My tears to smiles, my sad to glad. Amen.

—Anne Bradstreet

Speaking to yourselves in psalms and hymns and spiritual songs, singing and making melody in your heart to the Lord. Giving thanks always for all things unto God and the Father in the name of our Lord Jesus Christ.

Ephesians 5:19–20

Lord, how beautiful indeed are the feet that bring good news! I can't read the account of the women who visited your empty tomb without my heart beating a bit faster. As terrifying as the events preceding that first Easter morning were, how quickly utter grief turned into complete joy! Fill me with that joy, Lord. May it emanate from me and spread to others.

This is the day which the Lord hath made; we will rejoice and be glad in it.

Psalm 118:24

Earlier this week I took it upon myself to visit a local botanic garden. It is just minutes from my home, but I don't often think to go there. I went on a weekday this time, which meant that the park was much less crowded. I appreciated the solitude, and chose to walk a path that winds around a small lake and through pinewoods. The path is made of wood chips, and as I rounded a bend, I heard a crunching noise, as if someone else were walking and enjoying the bright day. I expected to encounter another hiker. Imagine my surprise when I instead found myself face to face with a deer! The doe looked at me with clear brown eyes, unafraid, and I tried to remain perfectly still. I do not think I exaggerate when I say that we shared a moment; then she regained herself and bounded away. I am so glad I made the effort to visit the botanic garden that day! Dear Lord, thank you for an encounter that filled my spirit. Thank you for this world.

Open my eyes that I may see
Glimpses of truth thou sendest me;
Place in my hands the wonderful key
That shall unclasp, and set me free:
Silently now I wait for thee,
Ready, my God, thy will to see;
Open my eyes, illumine me, Spirit divine!
Open my ears that I may hear
Voices of truth thou sendest clear;
And while the wavenotes fall on my ear,
Ev'rything false will disappear:
Silently now I wait for thee,
Ready my God, thy will to see;
Open my heart illumine me, Spirit divine!

—Clara H. Scott

Jesus saith unto him, I am the way, the truth, and the life: no man cometh unto the Father, but by me.

John 14:6

Only a few things are actually impossible. And this is one of them: to please God without faith, not faith in ourselves, but faith in him. We have to believe he exists, and that he rewards us for simply believing in him and desiring him. The reward, of course, is that we find him. This is what pleases him, that we would receive our hope and satisfaction in him. This is what has always pleased him, from Abraham until today: people who seek him with humility and joy.

*Be kindly affectioned one to another
with brotherly love; in honour
preferring one another.
Not slothful in business;
fervent in spirit; serving the Lord.
Rejoicing in hope; patient in tribulation;
continuing instant in prayer.
Distributing to the necessity of saints;
given to hospitality.*

Romans 12:10–13

Beloved, think it not strange concerning the fiery trial which is to try you, as though some strange thing happened unto you. But rejoice, inasmuch as ye are partakers of Christ's sufferings; that, when his glory shall be revealed, ye may be glad also with exceeding joy.

1 Peter 4:12–13

Most merciful God, the helper of all men, so strengthen us by thy power that our sorrow may be turned into joy, and we may continually glorify thy holy name; through Jesus Christ our Lord. Amen.

11th-century prayer

*The Lord liveth; and blessed
be my rock; and exalted be the God of
the rock of my salvation.*

2 Samuel 22:47

Whatever is right and pure,
excellent and gracious,
admirable and beautiful,
fill my mind with these things.
Too much of the world
comes to me in tones of gray and brown.
Too great the temptation
to indulge obsessive thoughts
and sordid plans.
Guard my mind;
place a fence around my motives.
The pure, the lovely, the good—Yes!
Only those today.

I will praise the name of God with a song,
and will magnify him with thanksgiving.

Psalm 69:30

My daughter Alexa, a high school student, loves to sing. She has been involved in choir since she was a little girl. Yesterday was Monday, and my daughter came home from school discouraged about a misunderstanding with a friend, and the fact that she had more homework than she'd anticipated. Every Monday evening is rehearsal time for the church choir Alexa is in. The kids meet for an hour or so to practice right after dinner. Usually she looks forward to it, but yesterday she didn't want to go. She felt tired and worried about her schoolwork. I encouraged her to go anyway, and promised that I'd be right there at the end of practice, ready to bring her back home. When I dropped my girl off, she looked positively glum. Imagine my surprise when I picked up a beaming, transformed daughter an hour later! "I can't believe I always forget how good this choir makes me feel!" Alexa enthused, and I had to smile. Lord, thank you for reminding me and my beloved daughter how praising you in song can uplift one's heart.

Happy is he that hath the God of Jacob for his help, whose hope is in the Lord his God. Which made heaven, and earth, the sea, and all that therein is: which keepeth truth for ever.

Psalm 146:5–6

Even them will I bring to my holy mountain, and make them joyful in my house of prayer: their burnt offerings and their sacrifices shall be accepted upon mine altar; for mine house shall be called an house of prayer for all people.

Isaiah 56:7

Looking unto Jesus the author and finisher of our faith; who for the joy that was set before him endured the cross, despising the shame, and is set down at the right hand of the throne of God.

Hebrews 12:2

Every word of God is pure:
he is a shield unto them
that put their trust in him.

Proverbs 30:5

I have a friend who has read the Bible from cover to cover, and she described it as a profound experience. I have not read the Bible in this manner; I have favorite verses but, truth be told, the biblical prose can be intimidating. I do not always understand how the verses apply to my broken dishwasher or sick pet. And there are so many interpretations, sometimes conflicting, of what is within the Bible's pages! God, grant me a clear, level head and an open heart so that I might understand the wise ways of your Word. May the rich stories, the adventures and drama, and instruction that the Bible has to offer, be accessible to me. May I have the wisdom to apply its contents to my day-to-day life, and may I always be open to your teachings.

For he shall not much remember the days of his life; because God answereth him in the joy of his heart.

Ecclesiastes 5:20

Bless us in this time of good fortune. Give us the grace to be grateful for newfound comforts, magnanimous among those who have less, and thoroughly giving with all we've been given. Amen.

Let the field be joyful, and all that is therein: then shall all the trees of the wood rejoice before the Lord: for he cometh, for he cometh to judge the earth: he shall judge the world with righteousness, and the people with his truth.

Psalm 96:12–13

Lord, on days when I'm privileged to be out walking in the beautiful world you created, I sometimes feel as if all the plants and animals are celebrating their creation with you. If only we humans were as joyful, it would be simply marvelous! Thank you, Lord, for the glory of your creation and the reminder it brings that this is truly your world, and you will return to redeem it.

I sing because I'm happy,
I sing because I'm free,
For His eye is on the sparrow,
and I know He watches me.

—Civilla D. Martin

I know also, my God, that thou triest the heart, and hast pleasure in uprightness. As for me, in the uprightness of mine heart I have willingly offered all these things: and now have I seen with joy thy people, which are present here, to offer willingly unto thee.

1 Chronicles 29:17

And in the days of these kings shall the God of heaven set up a kingdom, which shall never be destroyed: and the kingdom shall not be left to other people, but it shall break in pieces and consume all these kingdoms, and it shall stand for ever.

Daniel 2:44

Charge them that are rich in this world, that they be not highminded, nor trust in uncertain riches, but in the living God, who giveth us richly all things to enjoy. That they do good, that they be rich in good works, ready to distribute, willing to communicate.

1 Timothy 6:17–18

The people were anxious, and perhaps even afraid. The priest had taught the Law of God, and they had clearly failed. But their repentance made it a holy day, a day of restoration and renewal. This was cause for rejoicing, so Nehemiah commands them to celebrate, taking care to provide for those with nothing. Don't be sad, he says, because the joy of a restored relationship with God is your strength. Today is also a holy day, a day to repent, and then to celebrate God's forgiveness and love.

Then he said unto them, Go your way, eat the fat, and drink the sweet, and send portions unto them for whom nothing is prepared: for this day is holy unto our Lord: neither be ye sorry; for the joy of the Lord is your strength.

Nehemiah 8:10

And it shall be said in that day, Lo, this is our God; we have waited for him, and he will save us: this is the Lord; we have waited for him, we will be glad and rejoice in his salvation.

Isaiah 25:9

For his anger endureth but a moment; in his favour is life: weeping may endure for a night, but joy cometh in the morning.

Psalm 30:5

Joy will always return to those who love God. We may find ourselves brought low by some of life's difficulties—and certainly by the tragedies that take us by storm. But none of these—not even the tragedies—can rob us of the deep-seated joy we have in our God. We may weep, even as Jesus did at times, but like him, we have a future joy set before us that no struggle on this earth can undermine or destroy. Our morning lies just ahead.

For what thanks can we render to God again for you, for all the joy wherewith we joy for your sakes before our God.

1 Thessalonians 3:9

How excellent is thy lovingkindness, O God! therefore the children of men put their trust under the shadow of thy wings. They shall be abundantly satisfied with the fatness of thy house; and thou shalt make them drink of the river of thy pleasures.

Psalm 36:7–8

Lord, I often thank you for things that make me happy. If I'm enjoying the weather, I thank you. If I appreciate a good friendship, I thank you. A parking place, a cappuccino, a tax refund—these are blessings I rejoice in. But I don't want to overlook what's most important—that I find fullness of joy in your presence. So thank you, my wonderful Lord, for being you. And thank you for being with me.

Will tomorrow be less hectic and more inclined toward joy? Will I be less tired? God help me, I'm not waiting to find out. In your creation, joy can be found anytime, but mostly now. Keep reminding me that now is all of life I can hold at any moment. It cannot be banked, invested, hoarded, or saved. It can only be spent.

Let the floods clap their hands:
let the hills be joyful together.

Psalm 98:8

Lord, bless this time of recreation. May we see that it is much more than another form of employment. It is a time to pull back and relax, to honor a thing you highly value—after work: rest.

And the ransomed of the Lord shall return, and come to Zion with songs and everlasting joy upon their heads: they shall obtain joy and gladness, and sorrow and sighing shall flee away.

Isaiah 35:10

And these things write we unto you, that your joy may be full.

1 John 1:4

There can be no experience of joy without first having faith in God. Our faith acts as a trigger that frees us from the anxieties, worries, and concerns that bog down our happiness and keep our bliss blocked at its source. God is always ready to bless us, but it's first up to us to do our part to clear the way for those blessings to arrive. Then we get to know how it feels to live with joy.

Faith
in Prayer

May be able to comprehend with
all saints what is the breadth, and
length, and depth, and height; and
to know the love of Christ, which
passeth knowledge, that ye might be
filled with all the fullness of God.

Ephesians 3:18–19

From a child thou hast known the holy scriptures, which are able to make thee wise unto salvation through faith which is in Christ Jesus.

2 Timothy 3:15

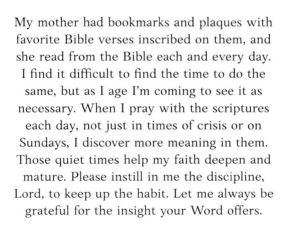

My mother had bookmarks and plaques with favorite Bible verses inscribed on them, and she read from the Bible each and every day. I find it difficult to find the time to do the same, but as I age I'm coming to see it as necessary. When I pray with the scriptures each day, not just in times of crisis or on Sundays, I discover more meaning in them. Those quiet times help my faith deepen and mature. Please instill in me the discipline, Lord, to keep up the habit. Let me always be grateful for the insight your Word offers.

Let us hold fast the profession of our faith without wavering. For he is faithful that promised.

Hebrews 10:23

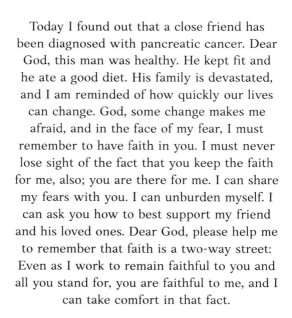

Today I found out that a close friend has been diagnosed with pancreatic cancer. Dear God, this man was healthy. He kept fit and he ate a good diet. His family is devastated, and I am reminded of how quickly our lives can change. God, some change makes me afraid, and in the face of my fear, I must remember to have faith in you. I must never lose sight of the fact that you keep the faith for me, also; you are there for me. I can share my fears with you. I can unburden myself. I can ask you how to best support my friend and his loved ones. Dear God, please help me to remember that faith is a two-way street: Even as I work to remain faithful to you and all you stand for, you are faithful to me, and I can take comfort in that fact.

A mighty fortress is our God,
a bulwark never failing;
our helper he, amid the flood
of mortal ills prevailing.

—Martin Luther,
trans. Frederick Hedge

I need thee ev'ry hour, most gracious Lord;

No tender voice like thine can peace afford.

I need thee ev'ry hour, stay thou near by;

Temptations lose their pow'r when thou art nigh.

I need thee ev'ry hour, in joy or pain;

Come quickly and abide, or life is vain.

I need thee ev'ry hour, teach me thy will;

Thy promises so rich, in me fulfill.

I need thee ev'ry hour, most Holy One

O make me thine indeed, thou blessed Son.

I need thee, o I need thee;

Ev'ry hour I need!

O bless me now, my Savior, I come to thee.

Amen.

—Annie S. Hawks

*He that overcometh, the same
shall be clothed in white raiment;
and I will not blot out his name
out of the book of life, but I will
confess his name before my Father,
and before his angels.*

Revelation 3:5

Lord, help me to resist temptation today
and hold fast to my faith. Help me to do the
right thing since you and your angels are
watching. So are my family and friends. If I
am faithful, you will clothe me with robes of
righteousness. My name will be in your book
of life. With your help, I can overcome.

The next day John seeth Jesus coming unto him, and saith, Behold the Lamb of God, which taketh away the sin of the world.

John 1:29

We hear this verse so often we sometimes fail to comprehend and appreciate it. It is not just a banner at a football game, however; it is an eternal, life-giving truth. God gave his own Son. If we believe that, we have an everlasting life. God's love leads to eternal life. Don't take this lightly. Nothing could be more important than this. Nothing could be more loving. Or more amazing.

I believe, God, that you give us faith
as a means of getting in touch
with your love. For once we have that
love, we can pass it on to others.

—Henry Drummond

O Lord my God, be not thou far from me; my God, have regard to help me; for there have risen up against me sundry thoughts, and great fears, afflicting my soul. How shall I pass through unhurt? How shall I break them to pieces? This is my hope, my one only consolation, to flee unto thee in every tribulation, to trust in thee, to call upon thee from my inmost heart, and to wait patiently for thy consolation. Amen.

—Thomas à Kempis

For the kingdom of God is not meat and drink; but righteousness, and peace, and joy in the Holy Ghost.

Romans 14:17

"Another close call," Bridget said glumly. Bridget is an actress, and she was referring to a recent audition in which she almost, but didn't, get a plum role. "But God has my back," she added, brightening. "I just need to be patient, and stay the course. I've got the skills. I work hard. My time will come!"

Dear Lord, it can be frustrating when I reach high and don't seem to succeed. Help me to be patient and remember that you work with us all our lives, just on your time!

Being confident of this very thing, that he which hath begun a good work in you will perform it until the day of Jesus Christ.

Philippians 1:6

O may thy spirit guide my feet
In ways of righteousness;
Make every path of duty straight,
And plain before my face.
Amen.

—Joachim Neander

To set up on high those that be low; that those which mourn may be exalted to safety.

Job 5:11

At the beginning of his great trial, the patriarch Job still has much to learn about God. But he does know this: God sets on high those who are low and exalts those who mourn. This truth helped Job endure his pain. It can help us, too. Ultimately, God alone ensures our safety and lifts us up when we humble ourselves before him. We have to believe that, especially when we hurt.

Even in the face of struggles and difficulties, there is a higher order of goodness at work in our lives. We may not be able to physically detect it at all times, but our faith knows the truth, and the truth sets us free.

God answers sharp and
sudden on some prayers.

And thrusts the thing we
have prayed for in our face,

A gauntlet with a gift in't.

—Elizabeth Barrett Browning

For thou wilt light my candle:
the Lord my God will enlighten my
darkness. As for God, his way
is perfect: the word of the Lord is
tried: he is a buckler to all those
that trust in him.

Psalm 18:28, 30

Lord, light my candle today. Enlighten my
darkness and let your light shine through
me. Your word is proven. Your strength is
sufficient. Let me show this to others, as I
speak of your promises and trust you to keep
them. Although my understanding is limited,
your ways are perfect. So be my candle and
my shield, and I will praise you.

Lord, thank you for the gift of prayer. What an amazing gift it is to be able to speak to you any time I need to. May I remember to not only seek you in times of need, but to thank you for all the blessings in my life. May my time in prayer bring me closer to you and help me be grateful for all the wonderful things in my life.

We plow the fields and scatter

The good seed on the land,

But it is fed and watered

By God's almighty hand;

He sends the snow in winter,

The warmth to swell the grain,

The breezes and the sunshine,

And soft, refreshing rain.

All good gifts around us

Are sent from heaven above:

Then thank the Lord, O thank the Lord

For all His love.

—Matthias Claudius

The Father loveth the Son, and hath given all things into his hand.

John 3:35

The Father has given all things into his Son's hand. All things include the Father's power and wisdom and mercy. The Son has the Father's words, and he has the Father's Spirit. That's why the Apostle John says if we believe in the Son, we have eternal life. Our faith in Jesus is rewarded because the Father loves the Son. And he loves us.

O Lord Jesus Christ, who didst give thy life for us that we might receive pardon and peace; mercifully cleanse us from all sin, and evermore keep us in thy favor and love, who livest and reignest with the Father and the Holy Spirit, ever one God, world without end. Amen.

6th-century prayer

Nevertheless my lovingkindness will I not utterly take from him, nor suffer my faithfulness to fail. My covenant will I not break, nor alter the thing that is gone out of my lips.

Psalm 89:33–34

Not all the psalms were written by King David. This one, for example, was written about King David by Ethan the Ezrahite. Ethan is comforted, as we should be, that God made and kept his promises to David. Even if David's sons "forsake my law, and walk not in my judgments" (verses 30–31), "my covenant will I not break," God says.

Actually, David's sons did fail to follow God. Most of them failed. But one of his descendants was Jesus. "I will not lie unto David. His seed shall endure for ever," Ethan writes (verses 35–36). God promises not to break his promises, and throughout all time believers have found comfort in this. "Blessed be the Lord for evermore," Ethan concludes.

Everything looks much brighter than it did before. My prayer for strength has been answered. My cries for help have been heard. My pleas for mercy flew directly to your throne. Now I'm ready to help my neighbor, Lord. Let me not delay.

If my people, which are called by my name, shall humble themselves, and pray, and seek my face, and turn from their wicked ways; then will I hear from heaven, and will forgive their sin, and will heal their land.

2 Chronicles 7:14

This is not just a promise to you. It's a promise to a group, to God's people, collectively and corporately. Your church or your family could learn to pray this way, with humility and repentance, and God will hear and heal. That's the promise. It is a great comfort that he hears my prayer. But he also hears our prayers. Can you pray with others today? Seek his face together.

Praised be You, my Lord, through our Sister Mother Earth, who sustains us, governs us, and who produces varied fruits with coloured flowers and herbs. Praised be You, my Lord, through Brother Wind and through the air, cloudy and serene, and every kind of weather. Praised be You, my Lord, through Sister Moon and the stars in heaven: you formed them clear and precious and beautiful. Praised be You, my Lord, through Brother Fire, through whom You light the night and he is beautiful and playful and robust and strong. Praised be You, my Lord, with all your creatures, especially Sir Brother Sun, who is the day and through whom you give us light. And he is beautiful and radiant with great splendors and bears likeness of You, Most High One.

—St. Francis of Assisi,
"The Canticle of Brother Sun"

Before prayer

I weave a silence on my lips,

I weave a silence into my mind,

I weave a silence within my heart.

I close my ears to distractions,

I close my eyes to attentions,

I close my heart to temptations.

Calm me, O Lord as you stilled the storm,

Still me, O Lord, keep me from harm.

Let all the tumult within me cease,

Enfold me Lord in your peace

—Celtic Traditional Prayer

Jesus saith unto him, Rise,
take up thy bed, and walk.

John 5:8

Sometimes I am afraid. Sometimes the path before me seems almost impossible. Last year, I decided to return to school. The office where I work indicated that I would have a better chance of advancing if I pursued a graduate degree. But I was anxious. School has never come easily to me, and at this stage of my life, I have myriad responsibilities, including a house and two active children under the age of five. But I prayed about it, and worked with my wife to figure out a humane course schedule that makes sense for our family. Though it will take a long time, I will eventually earn my degree. This first year I have been gratified to learn that I can keep up with my coursework and still make time for my job and family. It isn't always easy, though, and I pray for strength every day. I have learned that if I have faith, God will help me take on enormous challenges.

That the communication of thy faith may become effectual by the acknowledging of every good thing which is in you in Christ Jesus.

Philemon 1:6

Though Marilyn loves to sing, she sometimes can't stay in tune. When she was a child, her choir instructor would often tell her to "just mouth the words." Marilyn became shy about her voice; it wasn't until years later, when her boyfriend Erik came upon her singing hymns in the kitchen, that she was encouraged to express herself again in song. "Singing makes me happy," Marilyn says. "Erik reminded me that God doesn't care if I'm note perfect!" Dear Lord, you embolden us to speak out in many ways, one of which is the gift of song. May I never fear that my song is not sweet enough!

And at midnight Paul and Silas prayed, and sang praises unto God: and the prisoners heard them.

Acts 16:25

Pray without ceasing,

Let your love illumine the skies

That the darkness of man may drop away

And only the light of God show through.

Pray unto the Holy,

With all your heart and soul

Pray for the shining light of guidance

That your path may be glorious with love.

–St. Augustine

The Lord is nigh unto all them that call upon him, to all that call upon him in truth. He will fulfill the desire of them that fear him: he also will hear their cry, and will save them.

Psalm 145:18–19

The Lord is near. That is the great promise of faith. All we have to do is call and cry. That is the great promise of prayer. So many promises in scripture, including salvation itself, come by asking and believing. He is always near us. We draw near to him in prayer. And he fulfills "the desire of them that fear him."

Matthew Henry, the famous English Bible commentator, said, "Between the humble and contrite heart and the majesty of heaven there are no barriers: the only password is prayer." Prayer is the key to the lock, the channel of grace, the very gate of heaven. And thankfully, "The Lord is nigh unto all them that call upon him."

Lord, we've tossed our prayers aloft, and hopefully, expectantly, we wait for your answers. As we do, we will: listen, for you speak in the voice of nature; see you as a companion in the face and hand of a friend; feel you as a sweet-smelling rain, a river breeze; believe you can provide encouragement, direction, and guidance for those who have only to ask. We feel your presence.

*Thy statutes have been my songs
in the house of my pilgrimage.*

Psalm 119:54

In days of old, people would travel long
distances to make pilgrimages. Let me
turn my daily life into a pilgrimage
towards you, Lord. As I hike a trail, or
drive to the grocery store, or take a train
to visit my child at college, let me be
mindful that I continue traveling towards
you. Let me never forget that, wherever
my earthly journeys take me, you are my
goal and my ultimate destination!

The day was long, the burden I had borne
Seemed heavier than I could no longer bear;
And then it lifted—but I did not know
Someone had knelt in prayer.
Had taken me to God that very hour,
And asked the easing of the load, and He
In infinite compassion, had stooped down
And lifted the burden from me.
We cannot tell how often as we pray
For some bewildered one, hurt and distressed,
The answer comes, but many times these hearts
Find sudden peace and rest.
Someone had prayed, and faith, a lifted hand
Reached up to God, and He reached down that day.
So many, many hearts have need of prayer—
Then, let us, let us pray.

—Author Unknown

When my father and my mother forsake me, then the Lord will take me up.

Psalm 27:10

Sooner or later, we will feel forsaken. Someone we love will turn aside or fail to pay attention. Someone close to us may betray us or hurt us. But the Lord will take us up. He will gather us in his arms like lambs. He will teach us his ways. So, have courage. Be strong. He has not overlooked you or forsaken you. He will take you up.

Yes, Father in heaven, often have we found that the world cannot give us peace, O but make us feel that thou art able to give us peace; let us know the truth of thy promise: that the whole world may not be able to take away thy peace.

—Soren Kierkegaard

Lord, make me an instrument of your peace;

where there is hatred, let me sow love;

where there is injury, pardon;

where there is doubt, faith;

where there is despair, hope;

where there is darkness, light;

and where there is sadness, joy.

Divine Master, grant that I may not
so much seek to be consoled as to console;

to be understood as to understand;

to be loved as to love.

For it is in giving that we receive,

it is in pardoning that we are pardoned,

and it is in dying that we are born to eternal life.

—St. Francis of Assisi

But God will redeem my
soul from the power of the grave:
for he shall receive me.

Psalm 49:15

From the first book of the Bible to be written
down (Job) to the last words of Revelation,
God's power over death is assumed and
desired. Job said, "For I know that my
redeemer liveth, and that he shall stand at
the latter day upon the earth: And though
after my skin worms destroy this body, yet
in my flesh shall I see God" (Job 19:25–26).
In the resurrection we "shall be priests of
God and of Christ, and shall reign with him"
(Revelation 20:6).

The resurrection of Jesus ensures that "Death
is swallowed up in victory." "Oh, death,
where is thy sting?" the Apostle Paul asks (1
Corinthians 15:54–55). This promise, that we
will be with Jesus after death, is the central
tenet of Christianity, the "lively hope" to
which the Apostle Peter refers (1 Peter 1:3).
What greater promise could there be?

Rejoice evermore. Pray without ceasing. In every thing give thanks: for this is the will of God in Christ Jesus concerning you.

1 Thessalonians 5:16–18

Therefore I say unto you,
What things soever ye desire,
when ye pray, believe that ye receive
them, and ye shall have them.

Mark 11:24

It's not enough to pray for what we want.
We also have to believe God will hear us and
answer us. Prayer without faith is without
meaning, since faith is what pleases God.
He answers our prayers in his own time
and in his own way, of course, according
to his wisdom and mercy. But we can't get
impatient or lose heart, because that's not the
kind of prayer he hears. Just ask. And believe.

Call unto me, and I will answer thee, and show thee great and mighty things, which thou knowest not.

Jeremiah 33:3

O Lord, seek us, O Lord, find us
In Thy patient care;
Be Thy love before, behind us,
Round us, everywhere:
Lest the god of this world blind us,
Lest he speak us fair,
Lest he forge a chain to bind us,
Lest he bait a snare.
Turn not from us, call to mind us,
Find, embrace us, bear;
Be Thy Love before, behind us,
Round us everywhere.

—Christina Rossetti

My servant Moses is not so,
who is faithful in all mine house.

Numbers 12:7

I miss my parents, both of whom died within the last 10 years, but each day I strive to keep them alive—in my heart and in the world—by emulating the way they lived their lives. On days when I struggle, I remember my mother's kindness, my father's acts of service. I remember the day my dad and I shared coffee and talked about the qualities he admired in others: "Faith," he said, without hesitation. "Faith in God, in one's own path. From faith springs generosity of spirit." He went on to say that in the Bible, the stories of faith as embodied by men such as Moses lifted him. Dear God, may I persevere and have faith. Help me to remember that faithfulness is an attribute of great men like Moses, and within my reach as I strive to be my best self.

Embracing Joy

The people that walked in darkness
have seen a great light: they that
dwell in the land of the shadow of
death, upon them hath the light
shined.

Isaiah 9:2

For then shalt thou lift up thy face without spot; yea, thou shalt be stedfast, and shalt not fear.

Job 11:15

The distance between tears and joy is as brief as the summer. We sow in sorrow, clothed in dirt and sweat. Yet the Lord brings blackberries and tomatoes, the joy of harvest, and the giving of thanks. It is the law of the harvest, the promise of fresh food on a table of grace.

And yet this is merely a metaphor for the rhythm of our lives. By God's grace our joy will follow our tears as surely as the summer will follow the spring. The 19th-century preacher Charles Spurgeon put it this way: "When your eyes are dim with silver tears, think of the golden corn." When we are overwhelmed by the work to be done, we usually just have to wait for the seed to grow.

Thank you for each precious day,

For songs we sing and words we say,

For times of prayer and times of play.

Thank you for the sky and sun,

For days with clouds or days with none,

For the peace that comes when each day's done.

Thank you for your Spirit sent

To make straight the paths that have been bent

To watch over us in all events.

They on the rock are they,
which, when they hear, receive the
word with joy; and these have
no root, which for a while believe,
and in time of temptation fall away.

Luke 8:13

Does your word fall on good soil when I hear
it, Lord? Or does it fall on rocky ground?
Please help me cultivate my faith, so that it
does not wither in time of temptation. Let
my joy in you remain sharp and fresh.

Joy is not gush; joy is not jolliness.
Joy is perfect acquiescence in God's will
because the soul delights in God himself.

—H. W. Webb-Peploe

And they sing the song of Moses the servant of God, and the song of the Lamb, saying, Great and marvellous are thy works, Lord God Almighty; just and true are thy ways, thou King of saints.

Revelation 15:3

Considering how great our God is, a great king above all gods, we probably don't sing to him enough. Make a joyful noise today. Recall some hymn or worship song and sing it out loud. At least hum it as you work. Come before his presence with gratitude and joy. Sing unto the Lord. Every place he is, which is any place you are, he is the rock of your salvation. Praise him.

With grateful heart my thanks I bring,

before the great your praise I sing;

I worship in your holy place

and praise you for your truth and grace;

for truth and grace together shine

in your most holy word divine,

in your most holy word divine.

—"With Grateful Heart My Thanks I Bring"

Even before your birth, God instilled in you a strong spirit and an indomitable will to be a bright, shining light in the world. Turn that light on and shine! Let loose the joyful spirit that is you!

Before I formed thee in the belly I knew thee; and before thou camest forth out of the womb I sanctified thee.

Jeremiah 1:5

But when Jesus perceived their thoughts, he answering said unto them, What reason ye in your hearts? Whether is easier, to say, Thy sins be forgiven thee; or to say, Rise up and walk?

Luke 5:22–23

Lord, this is hard. I face different kinds of temptations and trials almost every day. But my faith is weak, and my patience is short. And you ask me to consider these tests a source of joy? I can't do this unless you help me. I can't do this unless I consider the outcome: more patience. But you will help me, or you wouldn't have asked me to do it. So, when I want to speak unkindly to a coworker or family member, guard my tongue. Remind me that I am becoming more patient. And more like you.

*Be glad in the Lord, and rejoice,
ye righteous: and shout for joy, all ye
that are upright in heart.*

Psalm 32:11

When I think of God, my heart is
so full of joy that the notes leap and
dance as they leave my pen: and since
God has given me a cheerful heart, I
serve him with a cheerful spirit.

—Franz Joseph Haydn

The heart of the prudent getteth knowledge; and the ear of the wise seeketh knowledge.

Proverbs 18:15

My wife and I had our first and only child, Amanda, later in life, and honestly, that child has been a gift in ways I never could have anticipated. One way our daughter has enriched my life is that, truly, she keeps me learning and growing. Amanda has such diverse interests. Through her, I've been introduced to anime movies, and new styles of music. She has even gotten me interested in the works of Edgar Allan Poe! These are areas I had never explored previously, and I appreciate being able to experience them with my child. Thank you, God, for the gift of a child who reminds me to never stop learning. May I always be a student of life.

*But whosoever drinketh of the water
that I shall give him shall never
thirst; but the water that I shall give him
shall be in him a well of water
springing up into everlasting life.*

John 4:14

Life has its difficult chapters. In the past two
years, both my parents died and my beloved
son struggled with his coursework, to the point
where he had to take a break from university.
He suffered through a period of confusion and
depression, and is still not sure if he will in
fact return to school. It's been a hard time for
my family, and yet amid the challenges, I have
enjoyed the support of my wife and a tightly knit
group of friends, one of whom helped my son get
a job that allows him to be self-reliant while he
decides on next steps. My life isn't "perfect," and
yet each morning I wake to a choice—how can
I embrace what is good on this day? How can
I tap into God within me, no matter what else
transpires? Lord, help me remember that external
circumstances cannot define my joy. Rather, joy
is something I can nurture within, even as I, and
those I love, experience ups and downs.

Go forth in the joy of the Lord, knowing how blessed you are. Celebrate the beauty of nature around you. Celebrate the goodness of fellowship with others. Celebrate the opportunity to grow and learn and take up the challenge of each new day. Most of all: Celebrate your life. How blessed you are!

But let all those that put their trust in thee rejoice: let them ever shout for joy, because thou defendest them: let them also that love thy name be joyful in thee.

Psalm 5:11

Whom having not seen, ye love; in whom, though now ye see him not, yet believing, ye rejoice with joy unspeakable and full of glory.

1 Peter 1:8

Wherefore, if God so clothe the grass of the field, which today is, and to morrow is cast into the oven, shall he not much more clothe you, O ye of little faith?

Matthew 6:30

Jesus seems almost incredulous here. How could we doubt the Father's care for us? He takes care of the lilies. Will he not take care of you? He is everywhere engaged with his creation. He feeds the ravens. He calms the seas. He sends the rain. The world is an object lesson of his interest in the details of our lives.

"I will give you the rain of your land in his due season, the first rain and the latter rain, that thou mayest gather in thy corn, and thy wine, and thine oil," he says (Deuteronomy 11:14). And so we rejoice "to the joy in harvest" (Isaiah 9:3). No wonder our Lord says, "O you of little faith."

Now the God of hope fills you with all joy and peace in believing that ye may abound in hope, through the power of the Holy Ghost.

Romans 15:13

May you rejoice in the written Word.
The scriptures can come alive for
you; only take, and read. Discover the
acts of God in history. Travel with his
disciples along the pathway of service.
See how his church began, how it
grew down through the centuries. Yes,
celebrate the written Word, for it is a
mirror of, and a witness to, the Living
Word of the heavens.

*Hitherto have ye asked nothing
in my name: ask, and ye shall receive,
that your joy may be full.*

John 16:24

Lord, I've asked for a lot. Teach me what it
means to ask in your name. So far, I have
wanted my life, or my friends' lives, to be
easier. But when I begin to pray in your
name, desiring your name to be honored and
your will to be done, that's when I can ask
and receive with confidence. I will receive
more than the thing I wanted. I will receive
it with greater joy knowing it is from you
and for your purposes. Help me to ask in
your name.

In this beautiful place, there are
wonders all around me, God, I know.
The only thing lacking is wonder.
Lift up my heart in praise!

My son, eat thou honey, because it is good; and the honeycomb, which is sweet to thy taste.

Proverbs 24:13

How grateful I am for the sweet things I eat! Of course, I don't want to overindulge, but I get so much enjoyment out of the sweet taste! Thank you, God, for creating sweet foods. Help me enjoy them in moderation and always praise you for the sweetness in my life.

May you enjoy all the streams of love that flow into your life: the love from family and friends; the love from parents and children; the love from pets and the love from God. Celebrate love all day long. For it is the breath of your existence, and the best of all reasons for living.

The steps of a good man are ordered by the Lord: and he delighteth in his way. Though he falls, he shall not be utterly cast down: for the Lord upholdeth him with his hand.

Psalm 37:23–24

Lord, help me to delight in your way. Help me to see each step as ordered by you. When I fall, hold my hand. This is what I need today. This is what I need every day. I need this certainty that I will not be cast down. And I need to delight in this certainty. When I have to make a tough decision today, help me to choose your path, because it always leads to joy.

May the blessing of light be on you, light without and light within. May the blessed sunshine shine on you and warm your heart till it glows like a great peat fire, so that the stranger may come and warm himself at it, and also a friend.

Traditional Irish Blessing

Blessed is the man that heareth me,
watching daily at my gates,
waiting at the posts of my doors.

Proverbs 8:34

Thou shalt raise up the foundations of many generations; and thou shalt be called, The repairer of the breach, The restorer of paths to dwell in.

Isaiah 58:12

Isaiah says the Messiah will be called the "Repairer of the Breach." Like walls that crumble and fortifications that fail, there are many broken relationships, broken promises, and broken lives. Gaps and rifts and fissures surround us, each filled with human pain. But Jesus came to mend them.

In the synagogue at Nazareth, Jesus said he came to heal the broken-hearted (Luke 4:16–20). He came "To appoint unto them that mourn in Zion, to give unto them beauty for ashes, the oil of joy for mourning, the garment of praise for the spirit of heaviness" (Isaiah 61:3). He came to repair the breach between man and God. And he can repair the breach between any of us.

O Lord, I savor this triumph: I met my goal! Day by day, I reached into my heart and found energy to keep on. Day by day, I reached out and found your hand leading, your inspiration guiding. Stand with me to accept applause for our joint success.

And now abideth faith, hope, charity, these three; but the greatest of these is charity.

1 Corinthians 13:13

As an adult with many demands on my time and energy, I am always interested in how to consistently achieve my potential and be my best self. For many years, I've enjoyed swimming as a way to stay healthy, both physically and emotionally. After a long day, a good swim clears my head, tones my muscles, and keeps me sharp and upbeat. Similarly, I've found that staying spiritually active has a positive effect on my outlook. Like exercise, staying spiritually engaged takes discipline—and sometimes I would rather just sit on the couch and eat chips! But when I make the effort, physical and spiritual exercise helps me to realize joy. Lord, please may I always remember that happiness can be part of the package when I develop my spiritual muscle. I can "work at" making joy a constant in my life.

The Lord thy God in the midst of thee is mighty; he will save, he will rejoice over thee with joy; he will rest in his love, he will joy over thee with singing. I will gather them that are sorrowful for the solemn assembly, who are of thee, to whom the reproach of it was a burden.

Zephaniah 3:17–18

Praise the Lord: ye heavens, adore Him;

Praise Him, angels in the height;

Sun and moon, rejoice before Him,

Praise Him, all ye stars of light.

. . .

Praise the God of our salvation;

Hosts on high, His power proclaim;

Heaven and earth and all creation,

Laud and magnify His Name.

—from The Foundling Hospital Collection
(1796), based on Psalm 148

He shall not fail nor be discouraged, till he have set judgment in the earth: and the isles shall wait for his law.

Isaiah 42:4

The Lord will not give up. There is much injustice on the earth, but he "will not fail nor be discouraged." The prophet is speaking here of Christ, "mine elect, in whom my soul delighteth" (verse 1). God finds joy in the perseverance of his son. We find joy in it too, since some of the injustice he confronts is in us.

Yet he confronts us gently: "He shall not cry, nor lift up, nor cause his voice to be heard in the street" (verse 2). What a patient, persistent Providence we serve, who waits for us with mercy and fills us with grace. Find joy in this: "I the Lord have called thee in righteousness, and will hold thine hand" (verse 6).

With boldness and wonder and
expectation, I greet you this morning,
God of sunrise and rising dew.
Gratefully, I look back to all that was
good yesterday and in hope, face
forward, ready for today.

Savior, teach me day by day,

Love's sweet lesson to obey;

Sweeter lesson cannot be,

Loving him who first loved me.

Teach me thus thy steps to trace,

Strong to follow in thy grace,

Learning how to love from thee,

Loving him who first loved me.

Thus may I rejoice to show

That I feel the love I owe;

Singing, till thy face I see,

Of his love who first loved me.

—Jane E. Leeson

*Every man according as he purposeth
in his heart, so let him give;
not grudgingly, or of necessity: for God
loveth a cheerful giver.*

2 Corinthians 9:7

The greatest blessing comes from giving.
When I give from the heart, I am doing
God's will and spreading the joy he has given
me. I am never left with less, because God
has this wonderful way of increasing my
blessings the more I share them with others.
Giving fills me with a sense of gratitude
for the mysterious workings of his miracles.
The more I give, the more he gives me to
give. How can I not stand in awe of such
a powerful God that recompenses me with
double the blessings I give away? God is
infinite goodness. His abundance doesn't run
out. I am grateful to be a channel for the flow
of God's blessings.

O come, let us sing unto the Lord: let us make a joyful noise to the rock of our salvation. Let us come before his presence with thanksgiving, and make a joyful noise unto him with psalms. For the Lord is a great God, and a great King above all gods. In his hand are the deep places of the earth: the strength of the hills is his also.

Psalm 95:1–4

Thou wilt shew me the path of life: in thy presence is fullness of joy; at thy right hand there are pleasures for evermore.

Psalm 16:11

And he brought forth his people with joy, and his chosen with gladness.

Psalm 105:43

Lord, why do other believers have such expressive joy when I don't? Is there something wrong with me? I keep hearing that we should have abundant lives, praising you all the time, but that doesn't ring true for me. Can I still love you without jumping for joy all the time? Still, I'd love to feel lighter in my faith—more simple smiles and fewer thoughtful scowls. Can I just enjoy your presence? That's what I want. Draw near to me, Lord, and teach me to smile.

Verily, verily, I say unto you, That ye shall weep and lament, but the world shall rejoice: and ye shall be sorrowful, but your sorrow shall be turned into joy.

John 16:20

O that thou hadst hearkened to my commandments! then had thy peace been as a river, and thy righteousness as the waves of the sea.

Isaiah 48:18

If we claim a promise we must face any condition attached to it. And many of the promises require our obedience to God. The peace of God is as full as a river, but it flows into the hearts of those who love him and obey him. This follows from our faith as naturally as a stream. God says, "Obey my voice, and I will be your God, and ye shall be my people" (Jeremiah 7:23). In this sense he is not the God of all people but only of those who obey him. Many of his promises are obtained through obedience, especially those promises that touch on our attitudes and dispositions: "If ye know these things, happy are ye if ye do them" (John 13:17).

Your soul can dance though the pain is here.

Call healing music to your ear.

Spot emotion's fickle turning,

Leap in love,

Stretch hopes,

Master fear's deep strains.

Dare to dance both health and pain.

However clumsy, long, or fleeting,

We dance life well if grace is leading.

Like an itch that won't let up, a buzz of creativity is catching our attention and wanting release. Songs whisper to us, wanting melodies; words and paintings are needing paper; dances, our moving feet. Help us recognize your presence in this nudge to movement.

Holding onto Hope

Which hope we have as an anchor of the soul, both sure and steadfast, and which entereth into that within the veil.

Hebrews 6:19

Dear God,
I pray today for your mercy and compassion.
I'm struggling with life, wrestling against it
and not allowing you to work your miracles
through me. I pray for a release from the
blocks that keep me from your love and
guidance. I pray for a stronger, deeper faith in
the perfection of my life, even if I can't make
sense of it right now. I pray for more spiritual
endurance and fortitude when I feel like giving
up. I pray, God, for your constant and loving
presence. Amen.

*Who is a God like unto thee, that
pardoneth iniquity, and passeth by the
transgression of the remnant of his
heritage? he retaineth not his anger for
ever, because he delighteth in mercy.
He will turn again, he will have
compassion upon us; he will subdue our
iniquities; and thou wilt cast all their
sins into the depths of the sea.*

Micah 7:18–19

How can I rejoice when I'm having "one of those days," Father? How can I pray continually when I feel overwhelmed?

When I look to Jesus' example, I find the answers I seek. He didn't stay on his knees 24/7, but he did maintain an ongoing dialogue with you. He acknowledged that he would prefer to avoid his cross, but he willingly took it up because it was necessary. He focused on the joy to come later, in due time.

I too can give thanks for the good things in my life, even when bad things are bearing down on me. I can keep up a dialogue with you as I go about my day, and I can be joyful in a deep abiding sense, knowing that all is in your hands.

Nevertheless we, according to his promise, look for new heavens and a new earth, wherein dwelleth righteousness.

2 Peter 3:13

Life can be challenging. It is imperfect. It can be ugly. I commute to work by train, and sometimes the litter I see by the side of the tracks saddens me—papers, plastic bags, abandoned toys, even once the rusted hulk of a car. We are not always good stewards of the world we live in, and while I believe it is important that we continue to try to repair and care for our earthly home, I also take comfort in the assurance of a shining life after this one. "New heavens and a new earth": that promise fills me with hope. Lord, thank you for reminding me that all will be made anew!

For I reckon that the sufferings of this present time are not worthy to be compared with the glory which shall be revealed in us. For the earnest expectation of the creature waiteth for the manifestation of the sons of God.

Romans 8:18–19

Dear God,

I've lost so much in the last few years. Friends and family have passed away. Dreams have come and gone. Finances have been a problem and I find myself losing hope. I ask in prayer for a renewal in my spirit. I know you never bring experiences into my life without a purpose, but please help me to stay in hope as I get through them and learn the lessons they are meant to give me. When everyone around me seems too busy and I am alone, be my constant friend and companion. When circumstances keep occurring that test my strength and soul, flood my heart with hope and refresh my mind with new solutions. I don't ask for an easy life, God, just that when things aren't so easy, I never, ever lose hope. Amen.

Wherefore gird up the loins of your mind, be sober, and hope to the end for the grace that is to be brought unto you at the revelation of Jesus Christ.

1 Peter 1:13

Earth has no sorrow that
Heaven cannot heal.

—Thomas Moore

There shall not any man be
able to stand before thee all the days
of thy life: as I was with Moses,
so I will be with thee: I will not fail
thee, nor forsake thee.

Joshua 1:5

After Moses died, Joshua was alone with a lot of responsibility. The Israelites had wandered in the wilderness. Now he would have to lead them into battle. They had come to the Promised Land, but someone else was living there. So God encouraged Joshua by promising to be with him, as he had been with Moses.

The promise had been given to the people who would follow God, in Deuteronomy 31:6. And what appears as a promise to one man becomes a promise to his people today in Hebrews 13:5: "For he hath said, I will never leave thee, nor forsake thee.'" Whatever challenges we face, that's good to know.

Lord Jesus Christ, in thee alone,
My only hope on earth I place,
For other comforter is none,
No help have I but in thy grace.
There is no man nor creature here,
No angel in the heav'nly sphere,
Who at my call can succor me.
I cry to thee,
In thee I trust implicitly.

—Johannes Schneesing,
trans. Catherine Winkworth

And he sent them to preach the kingdom of God, and to heal the sick. And he said unto them, Take nothing for your journey, neither staves, nor scrip, neither bread, neither money; neither have two coats apiece.

Luke 9:2–3

When we travel with God, we can travel lightly, knowing that our needs will be provided. When you send me out on a spiritual journey, Lord, let me be eager to go, heading on my way without expectation or reservation.

O Lord, enthroned in glory bright,
you reign above in heav'nly height;
the proud in vain your favor seek
but you have mercy for the meek;
through trouble though my pathway be,
you will revive and strengthen me,
you will revive and strengthen me.

—"With Grateful Heart My Thanks I Bring"

*But seek ye first the kingdom of
God, and his righteousness; and all
these things shall be added unto you.*

Matthew 6:33

What are all these things that will be added
if you seek the kingdom of God and his
righteousness? Jesus is talking about what we
eat and what we wear: ordinary, everyday
things we often worry about. But our Father
knows what we need. He feeds the birds and
clothes the fields with lilies. So don't worry.
He will take care of you.

A despairing heart mumbles,
"God is doing nothing."

A hopeful heart inquires, "God, what are
you going to do next?" and looks forward
to celebrating God's awesome ingenuity.

Lord,

I like the part about "new" and "better,"

But what's that going to look like? Feel like?

What's all this going to mean?

I want transformation,

But the change part scares me.

Give me strength, Lord.

Help me accept your gift of new life.

Lead me forward.

I put my trust in you.

Amen.

And our hope of you is steadfast, knowing that as ye are partakers of the sufferings, so shall ye be also of the consolation.

2 Corinthians 1:7

Why me, Lord? I have asked that question a million times, when I become ill, or one of my children is hurt. Why me, Lord? And his answer? Why not you? I learned the Lord doesn't pick and choose who suffers. We all suffer at some point in life, and no one is immune. But I also learned whatever suffering the Lord asks me to experience comes with the courage, strength, and compassion to get through it. It's a promise the Lord made to me, that he would never give me more than I could handle. So when things come into my life I'd rather not deal with, I have hope and faith that I can deal with them, with the Lord to guide me.

O Joy that seekest me through pain,

I cannot close my heart to thee;

I trace the rainbow through the rain,

And feel the promise is not vain

That morn shall tearless be.

—George Matheson,
"O Love That Wilt Not Let Me Go," verse 3

So here I am, waiting. I have answered your call to pray. I have heard your guidance—to sit tight. I have chosen quiet and rest because that is your will for me now. I am sitting on the sidelines, watching the hectic pace around me. I am finding contentment in the little blessings that flow into my days. I am trying to see all these things as big blessings because they come from you. But when can I get going again? When will I do the great works I've envisioned? When will the situation require dedicated action once again? When will I hear the trumpet call? When will I finally move onward and upward? I'm ready, Great Spirit! Here I am . . . waiting.

And now, O Lord God, thou art that God, and thy words be true, and thou hast promised this goodness unto thy servant.

2 Samuel 7:28

King David is talking here, grateful for God giving him a kingdom and keeping his promises. But you don't need a kingdom to know this is true. God is God. His words are true, and he has promised good things to his servants. If you are one of them, there's not much more to say. This is all you need, today or any day: his words are true.

I will praise thee; for I am fearfully and wonderfully made: marvellous are thy works; and that my soul knoweth right well.

Psalm 139:14

We are, as the Psalmist says, wondrously made. So much so, loving Creator, that by changing our minds we might be able to change our lives. It's the simple power of as if. Living as if we are going to fail, we often do. Living as if we are going to succeed, we often can. Keep us from being like teams who know the plays but doubt they can run them. Instead, we'll use your amazing gift of attitude, knowing you treat us as if we deserve your promised abundant life.

On our way to rejoicing, gladly let us go.

Christ our Lord has conquered;
vanquished is the foe.

Christ without, our safety;
Christ within, our joy;

Who, if we be faithful, can our hope destroy?

On our way rejoicing; as we forward move,

hearken to our praises, O lest God of love!

Unto God the Father joyful songs we sing;

unto God the Savior thankful hearts we bring;

unto God the Spirit bow we and adore,

on our way rejoicing now and evermore.

On our way rejoicing; as we forward move,

Hearken to our praises, O blest God of love!

—John S. Monsell

But know that the Lord hath set apart him that is godly for himself: the Lord will hear when I call unto him.

Psalm 4:3

With so much praying going on in the world, I wonder if God really hears my prayers. The psalmist had no doubt here, saying with certainty that the Lord will hear when called upon. It's a comfort to know that the God of the universe is not too busy or distracted to attentively bend his ear toward me. God is listening and is present in my life.

And God shall wipe away all tears from their eyes; and there shall be no more death, neither sorrow, nor crying, neither shall there be any more pain: for the former things are passed away.

Revelation 21:4

Dear Lord,

It's hard to face the day with hope, love and faith when all I see on the morning news are stories of death and violence. Even if I don't watch, I hear about it from friends, see it on social networks and at my workplace. I pray for a powerful faith to hold onto as I try to understand why there is so much pain and suffering in the world. I pray for a steadfast awareness of your presence, and that there is a bigger picture behind the smaller pieces of life I see. Only you, Lord, know what that bigger picture is. I pray for the trust and the faith to live my life in love and light, despite any darkness around me. Amen.

Hast thou faith? have it to thyself before God. Happy is he that condemneth not himself in that thing which he alloweth.

Romans 14:22

Lord, give me hope,
Give me patience to cope
And a reason to keep on trying.
Take my trembling hand
Give me power to stand
And a faith that is strong and undying.

He giveth power to the faint;
and to them that have no might
he increaseth strength.

Isaiah 40:29

Lord, I'm weak today. I'm not sure how much more I can do. Give me strength today, Lord. You come alongside those who are weary and faint. Come alongside me. You are the Everlasting God. I know you don't get tired or give up. I know you lift your people on eagles' wings. So, renew my strength. And I will praise you.

O Lord, hear my prayer for all who are in trouble this day.

Comfort those who are facing the loss of a loved one. After the wrenching grief, let their lonely hours be filled with fond memories of days gone by.

Strengthen those who are passing their days without work. During this time of financial stress, give them energy to make their employment the job of finding new work.

Encourage those who are finding it difficult to believe in the future. Let your hope fill their hearts as they recall all your past faithfulness. Show them that while there is life there is hope, that change is the only constant, and that change for the better is so likely.

Console those who are looking at all the negative aspects of life and finding it depressing. May they find joy in just one moment at a time. And may that be enough for now.

In all these ways I ask your blessing upon those in trouble. And please include me in that blessing, too!

Today I need your help, God, feeling the
need for a breath of fresh air. The old
habits and attitudes I've clung to for so
long seem stale and worn out. Renew me
from the inside out, starting now!

As a parent, what I wish for my daughter Anne is an easy path. When she struggles with her studies or experiences conflicts with friends, my heart aches. I know, however, that no one can be shielded from pain indefinitely, and that it is adversity as well as our joys and successes that shape us. My grandfather used to say that misfortune can build character, and I see that in my daughter: Challenges have shown her that she possesses an inner steel, even as they've demanded she develop patience and compassion. Dear Lord, help me to guide Anne so that she might meet hardship with strength, patience, and grace. May adversity help her to grow as a person.

But and if ye suffer for righteousness' sake, happy are ye: and be not afraid of their terror, neither be troubled.

1 Peter 3:14

In the dead of winter, God of springtimes, I'm gardening. Carrot tops rooting, sweet potatoes vining. I don't doubt the outcome since I've learned at your knee to live as if. As if useless can become useful; as if seemingly dead can live; as if spring will come.

With Solomon, I will rejoice.

For, lo, the winter is past, the rain is over and gone.
The flowers appear on the earth; the time of the singing of birds is come, and the voice of the turtle is heard in our land.
The fig tree putteth forth her green figs, and the vines with the tender grape give a good smell. Arise, my love, my fair one, and come away.

Song of Solomon 2:11–13

Uphold me according unto thy word, that I may live: and let me not be ashamed of my hope.

Psalm 119:116

Let thy mercy, O Lord, be upon us,
according as we hope in thee.

Psalm 33:22

Mercy and hope are related. If you need mercy today, then hope in God, for he is merciful. His loving-kindness is sufficient for your needs. His mercy gives you hope as you look to him with confidence and expectation. The more hope you have, the more mercy you receive. You experience it in concrete and tangible ways as you see God's care for you. Then your hope will increase.

To whom God would make known what is the riches of the glory of this mystery among the Gentiles; which is Christ in you, the hope of glory.

Colossians 1:27

We come, needing your help to move beyond the times we hurt one another and the times we willingly misunderstand, cherishing our differences, and the times we assume we know all there is to know about each other and turn away. And then there are the times that we make private rules only to publicly condemn anyone who fails to abide by them, limiting one another by labeling, interpreting, conditioning, insisting, resisting, defining. From all this, Lord, we come, asking that you forgive us as we forgive those "others" we need new eyes to see and ears to hear. Be with us as we do so.

*Now faith is the substance
of things hoped for,
the evidence of things not seen.*

Hebrews 11:1

And so, after he had patiently endured, he obtained the promise.

Hebrews 6:15

Abraham is set before us as an example of one who inherited the promises of God. And in this case the promise was unconditional. God said he would bless Abraham and multiply him and make his name great. In fact, he said it several times.

We are told here to imitate those "followers of them who through faith and patience inherit the promises" (verse 12). God does what he says but may do it on his own time or even in stages, as he did with Abraham (Genesis 12:3, 15, 22:17). As Abraham learned, it was because of God's character that we "have a strong consolation, who have fled for refuge to lay hold upon the hope set before us" (Hebrews 6:18). Sometimes we just wait.

But they know not the thoughts of the Lord, neither understand they his counsel: for he shall gather them as the sheaves into the floor.

Micah 4:12

Last year, an old college friend called with the devastating news that after 23 years of marriage, her husband had admitted to a longstanding affair and asked for a divorce. My friend had felt secure in her husband's love, and was blindsided by this betrayal. In the months since, she has taken comfort in the community of her church, and found solace in her faith. "It's true: sometimes people disappoint us," she told me recently. We'd met for lunch, and though she spoke wryly, she looked and sounded better than she had in months. "But God is always faithful to us." I was struck by her words, and on the walk home pondered the resilience that grows when we know someone has our back. Dear Lord, help me to remember that you are a constant in my life, in times of joy but also adversity.

God is faithful, by whom ye were called unto the fellowship of his Son Jesus Christ our Lord.

1 Corinthians 1:9

Today may you come to acceptance. What is, is. May you find blessed relief in seeing—without judging, being—without having to become, knowing—without needing to change a thing. Then, should you be healed, it will be a gracious, unexpected surprise. May you soon arrive at perfect acceptance.

I can be afraid, but God gives me strength to act anyway. I can be uncertain, but God gives me a foundation that is firm and unyielding to stand upon.

By faith Noah, being warned of God of things not seen as yet, moved with fear, prepared an ark to the saving of his house; by which he condemned the world, and became heir of the righteousness which is by faith.

Hebrews 11:7

He that hath an ear, let him hear what the Spirit saith unto the churches; To him that overcometh will I give to eat of the hidden manna, and will give him a white stone, and in the stone a new name written, which no man knoweth saving he that receiveth it.

Revelation 2:17

Lord,

Give me hope for times when all seems hopeless. Give me strength for times when my own human weakness brings me down. Give me love when I feel alone and lost and misunderstood. I ask in prayer for a powerful sense of hope as I go forward to face my day. I know I'll face challenges, especially with other people. I know things won't always go my way. I know the news of the world will try to bring me to my knees. But hope, my Lord, will be the wings that keep me soaring when gravity tries to pull me back to the ways of the world, and the arms that hold me up when my own begin to fail me. Give me hope, Lord. Amen.

The Lord is good unto them that wait for him, to the soul that seeketh him. It is good that a man should both hope and quietly wait for the salvation of the Lord.

Lamentations 3:25–26

For we are saved by hope: but hope that is seen is not hope: for what a man seeth, why doth he yet hope for? But if we hope for that we see not, then do we wait with patience for it.

Romans 8:24–25

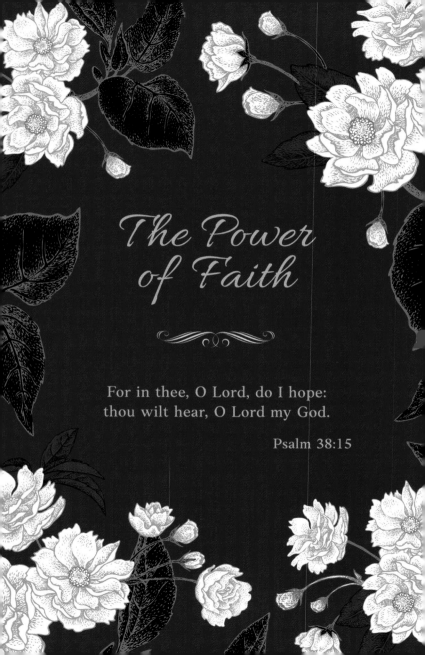

The Power of Faith

For in thee, O Lord, do I hope:
thou wilt hear, O Lord my God.

Psalm 38:15

May God, who seeth all things, and who is the ruler of all spirits and the Lord of all flesh—who chose our Lord Jesus Christ and us through him to be a peculiar people—grant to every soul that calleth upon his glorious and holy name, faith, peace, patience, long-suffering, self-control, purity, and sobriety, to the well-pleasing of his name, through our High Priest and Protector, Jesus Christ, by whom be to him glory, and majesty, and power, and honor, both now and forevermore.

—Clement of Rome

You are my strength, my shield, my rock,

my fortress strong against each shock,

my help, my life, my tower,

my battle sword,

almighty Lord—

Who can resist your power?

—Adam Reissner,
trans. Catherine Winkwohrt

For the Lord will not forsake his people for his great name's sake: because it hath pleased the Lord to make you his people.

1 Samuel 12:22

For the ancient Hebrews, and for the church today, this is an amazing truth: it pleased the Lord to make us his people. Because of this, he will not forsake us. His own reputation is at stake. He has put his name on us. Our faithfulness conveys a sense of his power and majesty to everyone who sees how he loves us and provides for us. We are his people, and he loves us.

Only faith can look past a seemingly impossible situation and believe that it will change. I believe you are a God of miracles, Lord. These are days of miracles, as were the days of Noah, Moses, and Joseph. I may not see the seas parted, peoples freed, or congregations caught up to heaven, but through faith I expect wonderful gifts from you. I believe that with you, all things are possible!

*And the apostles said unto the Lord,
Increase our faith. And the Lord
said, If ye had faith as a grain of
mustard seed, ye might say unto this
sycamine tree, Be thou plucked up
by the root, and be thou planted in
the sea; and it should obey you.*

Luke 17:5–6

For God so loved the world, that he gave his only begotten Son, that whosoever believeth in him should not perish, but have everlasting life.

John 3:16

I am a hospice nurse, and have seen in my work how the instinct to cling to life is strong. As a Christian, I believe that I can look forward to everlasting life after my time on Earth, but I imagine that when my time does come, it will be hard to let go of the life I know, populated by those I love. It is ironic and yet compelling that we cling to a temporary life on Earth, which is but a glimmer of what eternal life in heaven will be. Lord, help me to appreciate the transient beauty of life on Earth, even as I remember and embrace your promise of heaven and life everlasting.

To be with God, there is no need to be continually in church. We may make [a chapel] of our heart wherein to return from time to time to converse with him in meekness, humility, and love. There is not in the world a kind of life more sweet and delightful than that of a continual conversation with God.

—Brother Lawrence

God is our refuge and strength, a very present help in trouble. Therefore will not we fear, though the earth be removed, and though the mountains be carried into the midst of the sea. Though the waters thereof roar and be troubled, though the mountains shake with the swelling thereof. Selah. The Lord of hosts is with us; the God of Jacob is our refuge. Selah.

Psalm 46:1–3, 7

Hearken, my beloved brethren, Hath not God chosen the poor of this world rich in faith, and heirs of the kingdom which he hath promised to them that love him?

James 2:5

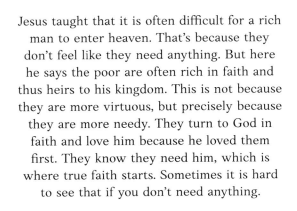

Jesus taught that it is often difficult for a rich man to enter heaven. That's because they don't feel like they need anything. But here he says the poor are often rich in faith and thus heirs to his kingdom. This is not because they are more virtuous, but precisely because they are more needy. They turn to God in faith and love him because he loved them first. They know they need him, which is where true faith starts. Sometimes it is hard to see that if you don't need anything.

Keep me at evening,
Keep me at morning,
Keep me at noon,
I am tired,
astray and stumbling,
shield me from sin.

Celtic Traditional Prayer

God with me lying down,
God with me rising up,
God with me in each ray of light
Nor I a ray of joy without Him,
Nor one ray without Him.
Christ with me sleeping,
Christ with me waking,
Christ with me watching,
Every day and night,
Each day and night.
God with me protecting,
The Lord with me directing,
The Spirit with me strengthening,
Forever and for evermore,
Ever and evermore,
Amen.

Celtic Prayer

For the promise, that he should be the heir of the world, was not to Abraham, or to his seed, through the law, but through the righteousness of faith.

Romans 4:13

How good to know our inheritance is secured by God's promises, not through keeping his commandments. We should obey him, of course. But the righteousness that matters comes by believing his promises. People who believe are people who obey. God's grace does not require the obedience of Abraham, but the faith of Abraham. Believe God and his promises. The rest follows.

Let not mercy and truth forsake thee: bind them about thy neck; write them upon the table of thine heart. So shalt thou find favor and good understanding in the sight of God and man.

Proverbs 3:3–4

God,

Give me the wisdom to know what
is important in life, and the courage
to pursue those things. My life is
such a blur lately, with an overload of
obligations, information and distractions
coming at me to the point where I end
up feeling so tired and worn down. I'm
not getting things done, and failing to
take care of my own health. Help me
slow down and focus, and not be afraid
to say no. Give me strength to tackle the
important duties, which then leave room
for more fun in my life. Show me, God,
balance and harmony between what I
need to do for others, and what I need to
replenish myself. Amen.

*That he would grant you,
according to the riches of his glory,
to be strengthened with might by
his Spirit in the inner man.*

Ephesians 3:16

But without faith it is impossible to please him: for he that cometh to God must believe that he is, and that he is a rewarder of them that diligently seek him.

Hebrews 11:6

If thou shalt confess with thy mouth the Lord Jesus, and shalt believe in thine heart that God hath raised him from the dead, thou shalt be saved.

Romans 10:9

Salvation is simple: Just confess and believe. If you believe Jesus died for your sins and was raised from the dead, you will be saved. And if you really believe it, you will be willing to say so. Out loud. It is simple, but not always easy. One reason we go to church is because it is easier there to sing songs and talk about the things we believe. But we also have opportunities to speak up at work or school. Our words should reflect our hearts. Confess and believe.

My brethren, count it all joy when ye fall into divers temptations. Knowing this, that the trying of your faith worketh patience. But let patience have her perfect work, that ye may be perfect and entire, wanting nothing.

James 1:2–4

I can do all things through Christ which strengtheneth me.

Philippians 4:13

My parents' deaths effected a profound transition for me. My mother died when I was 30 years old, and my father died this year, less than two years after we lost Mom. I am an adult, a single dad, and though I have been self-sufficient for years, I deeply miss being able to call my parents for counsel when faced with life's challenges. Mom and Dad were always there to support me and my son Evan. Since their deaths, I have sometimes felt alone as I've tried to navigate the challenges of parenting and make decisions about the future. Just last week, I met with my financial planner to adjust the college savings plan I am pursuing for my son. I wished I could call Dad to talk through the options. But I prayed about it, and slept on it, and when I woke the next morning, I had made a decision and felt at peace. God, you are there: Please help me to remember this, and that my strength to face life's trials comes from you.

Each prayer is a message of faith in God. We are saying, "I trust you; lead me. I believe in you; guide me. I need you; show me." When we offer ourselves openly, he will always answer.

*Come unto me, all ye that
labour and are heavy laden,
and I will give you rest.*

Matthew 11:28

We wander like children lost in a cave,
perilously close to the edge of despair.
Unable to see where we're going, we
crouch in fear rather than risk falling
while searching for an exit. Nudge us
beyond fear; send us guides who have
traveled dark passages before.

He that hath my commandments, and keepeth them, he it is that loveth me: and he that loveth me shall be loved of my Father, and I will love him, and will manifest myself to him.

John 14:21

May you be made perfect today—with the ability to see clearly your own imperfections, to accept them fully, and to try with all your heart to transform them for the good.

Therefore say, Thus saith the Lord God; Although I have cast them far off among the heathen, and although I have scattered them among the countries, yet will I be to them as a little sanctuary in the countries where they shall come.

Ezekiel 11:16

The Hebrews are in exile, but God says he will "be to them as a little sanctuary." Whenever we feel isolated and awkward, surrounded by people we do not know or things we do not understand, he is himself our sanctuary. He is our small but safe and sacred place.

Let the simple life take you by the hand today, and seek the goodness that only God can put in your heart. Be blessed and warmed in his life-giving presence!

Lord of my heart, give me a refreshing drink from the fountains of your love, walking through this desert as I have. Lord of my heart, spread out before me a new vision of your goodness, locked into this dull routine as I was. Lord of my heart, lift up a shining awareness of your will and purpose, awash in doubts and fears though I be.

A good man sheweth favor, and lendeth: he will guide his affairs with discretion. Surely he shall not be moved forever: the righteous shall be in everlasting remembrance. He shall not be afraid of evil tidings: his heart is fixed, trusting in the Lord. His heart is established, he shall not be afraid, until he sees his desire upon his enemies. He hath dispersed, he hath given to the poor; his righteousness endureth for ever; his horn shall be exalted with honor.

Psalm 112:5–9

Perhaps you remember a man or woman who was generous, discreet, and kind, a faithful person who was steady and fearless. We remember such people. God remembers them too. Determine to be such a person. Fix your heart on the Lord and his mercy. Be more like him. Then your strength and kindness will also be remembered. The Lord will honor you. It is a promise.

Dear Lord, I need renewal in my life.

But tell me what you want me to be, first,

then tell me what you want me to do.

Speak, for I am listening,

Guide, for I am willing to follow.

Be silent, for I am willing to rest in your love.

Today I want to spend time with you, Renewing Spirit.

In fact, I'd like to spend the whole day just being in your presence.

For this one day I will not worry about the work I have to do or the goals I want to accomplish.

I will pull back and simply listen for your guidance.

I'm willing to change my life in order to fit your perfect will, and I ask that you begin that work in my heart, even now.

I'll let go of personal ambition, for now.

I'll loosen my grip on the things I've wanted to accomplish and the recognition I've craved for so long.

All of this I give over to you.

I'm content to be a servant for now, quiet and unnoticed, if that is what you desire.

I'm even willing to be misunderstood, if you will only respond to my sincere prayer for a renewed heart.

Thank you. I need you so much.

That the blessing of Abraham might come on the Gentiles through Jesus Christ; that we might receive the promise of the Spirit through faith.

Galatians 3:14

In his letter to Galatia, Paul warns about the danger of trying to do through our effort what God wants us to do through faith. He is concerned that the Galatians are losing sight of the freedom and simplicity of the Gospel. Abraham was blessed, he says, for believing the promises of God. This is how we are blessed too, receiving the Spirit through faith. The righteous shall live by faith, he tells them. That is God's plan.

I wish to be of service, Lord. So give me courage to put my own hope and despair, my own doubt and fear at the disposal of others. For how could I ever help without first being, simply . . . real?

Blessings upon you. The blessing of perfect acceptance in the face of daunting circumstances. The blessing of contentment and peace while the winds blow and the waves rise higher and higher.

Blessings upon you. The blessing of knowing when acceptance must turn to action for the sake of all concerned. The blessing of strength to forsake contentment and peace for the purpose of comforting another.

Blessings upon you. The blessing of discernment: to recognize when to wait, and to understand when to move.

By faith he sojourned in the land of promise, as in a strange country, dwelling in tabernacles with Isaac and Jacob, the heirs with him of the same promise.

Hebrews 11:9

Abraham's faith motivated him to go to a new place and experience new blessings. Where will your faith lead you today? You can live in a land of promise, no matter how strange the world around you or how temporary your situation. You can find comfort from others who believe the same promises. So go into unfamiliar territory today with confidence and joy.

Faith is a true sign of bravery. It is looking forward to the future despite challenges and adversity; it is trusting in something that you can neither see nor touch yet knowing it is always there guiding you along life's path.

Understanding is the reward of faith. So do not seek to understand in order to believe, but believe so that you may understand.

—St. Augustine

For the Lord loveth judgment, and forsaketh not his saints; they are preserved for ever: but the seed of the wicked shall be cut off.

Psalm 37:28

The Lord does not forsake his saints, which is good to know when we are discouraged or overwhelmed. He will come to us and be with us. But he also loves judgment, which is just as amazing. Ultimately if not immediately, he takes our side against the wicked. In our day to day struggles we may not see it, but we need to remember it. He loves judgment. He takes sides. The good guys win, and he does not forsake us.

The Spirit of the Lord God is upon me; because the Lord hath anointed me to preach good tidings unto the meek; he hath sent me to bind up the brokenhearted, to proclaim liberty to the captives, and the opening of the prison to them that are bound.

To proclaim the acceptable year of the Lord, and the day of vengeance of our God; to comfort all that mourn.

To appoint unto them that mourn in Zion, to give unto them beauty for ashes, the oil of joy for mourning, the garment of praise for the spirit of heaviness; that they might be called trees of righteousness, the planting of the Lord, that he might be glorified.

Isaiah 61:1–3

All glory be to thee, Most High,
to thee all adoration.
In grace and truth thou drawest nigh
to offer us salvation.
Thou showest thy goodwill to men,
and peace shall reign on earth again;
we praise thy name forever.

Traditional hymn

Know therefore that the Lord
thy God, he is God, the faithful
God, which keepeth covenant and
mercy with them that love him
and keep his commandments to a
thousand generations.

Deuteronomy 7:9

God, it's easier to express gratitude
for your love when things are going
well than when I'm dealing with tough
issues. But even when I can't rely on
anything else, I can rely on your love.
I thank you for how you stand by me
even in times of trouble.

God be in my head,
and in my understanding;
God be in my eyes,
and in my looking;
God be in my mouth,
and in my speaking;
God be in my heart,
and in my thinking;
God be at my end,
and at my departing.

Old Sarum Primer

I will love thee, O Lord, my strength. The Lord is my rock, and my fortress, and my deliverer; my God, my strength, in whom I will trust; my buckler, and the horn of my salvation, and my high tower.

Psalm 18:1–2

Rock, fortress, deliverer, shield, horn, tower: Wow, that's a lot! But God's strength is all of these. If you need a place to stand today, or a place to hide, your trust in God is more than sufficient to protect you and encourage you. Any one of these would be enough, but you get them all. Because the Lord is your strength.

My God, how endless is your love!
Your gifts are every evening new,
and morning mercies from above
gently distill, like earthly dew.
You spread the curtains of the night,
great Guardian of my sleeping hours;
your sovereign Word restores the light,
and quickens all my drowsy powers.
I yield my powers to your command;
to you I consecrate my days:
perpetual blessings from your hand
demand perpetual songs of praise.

—Isaac Watts

Nurturing
Hope

Afterward shall the children of Israel
return, and seek the Lord their God,
and David their king; and shall fear
the Lord and his goodness in the
latter days.

Hosea 3:5

Dear God, complaints sometimes come first before I can feel free to love you. Sometimes you seem distant and unreasonable, uncaring. Help me understand why life can be so hurtful and hard. Hear my complaints and, in the spirit of compassion, show me how to move through pain to rebirth.

Gracious and healing God, thank you for everything you have done for me in the past.

You have restored me in unexpected ways and I will never be the same.

Thank you for being with me in the present and for the bright future you have planned for me. I pray for those who don't know you yet, who don't understand how you bless them again and again.

Use me to share the gratitude I feel, that others may grow to know you and your power.

In the name of Jesus, who healed the sick and made the lame to walk, I pray.

Amen.

O Holy Creator, who hath bound together heaven and earth, let me walk through your kingdom comforted and protected by the warm rays of your love. Let me be healed as I stand basking in the divine light of your presence, where strength and hope and joy are found. Let me sit at rest in the valley of your peace, surrounded by the fortress of your loving care.

Blessed is the man that endureth temptation: for when he is tried, he shall receive the crown of life, which the Lord hath promised to them that love him.

James 1:12

To spend my life with God is a choice I freely make. To love God and let God love me is the light of my life—what enables me to choose wisely and be thoughtful to those around me. God empowers me to resist temptation in the same breath that he compels me to give generously of my resources and myself. The blessing that James promises feels to me like God's love: It shines on me every day, lights the darkness, and illuminates my path.

For I know the thoughts that I think toward you, saith the Lord, thoughts of peace, and not of evil, to give you an expected end. Then shall ye call upon me, and ye shall go and pray unto me, and I will hearken unto you.

Jeremiah 29:11–12

In a silent world, no voice is heard,
No bark of a dog or song of a bird,
No strains of music or chime of a bell;
A noiseless, mysterious place to dwell.
But there is hope in this daunting place,
And happiness comes to a deaf child's face,
When, with his hands, his thoughts he can share,
He has learned to sign, because you are there.
You lift a cloud from the youngster's heart,
And she can smile because you did your part.
You've lightened the load she has to bear.
It isn't as hard, because you are there.
The smile on your face greets them each day.
Your simple gestures chase their fears away.
The love that you give shows them you care.
Their world is better, because you are there.

For the Lamb which is in the midst of the throne shall feed them, and shall lead them unto living fountains of waters: and God shall wipe away all tears from their eyes.

Revelation 7:17

But the God of all grace, who hath called us unto his eternal glory by Christ Jesus, after that ye have suffered a while, make you perfect, stablish, strengthen, settle you.

1 Peter 5:10

It's pretty clear we're not perfect yet. But God can make us whole and mature, and he will do it after we have suffered. That's what suffering is for. It makes us depend on him. As we do, we are established, strengthened, and settled by him. It's only then we know it is by his grace and for his glory. Otherwise, we would think we did it on our own, without his help. But he is the one who makes us whole.

Make us, O Lord, to flourish like pure lilies in the courts of thine house, and to show forth to the faithful the fragrance of good words, and the example of a Godly life, through thy mercy and grace. Amen.

7th-century prayer

But is now made manifest by the appearing of our Saviour Jesus Christ, who hath abolished death, and hath brought life and immortality to light through the gospel.

2 Timothy 1:10

By terrible things in righteousness wilt thou answer us, O God of our salvation; who art the confidence of all the ends of the earth, and of them that are afar off upon the sea.

Psalm 65:5

When we doubt your miracle-making power, Lord, show us the ordinary miracles of seasons, of hope regained, of love from family and friends, and of surprises that turn out miraculous simply by remaking our lives.

It is of the Lord's mercies that we are not consumed, because his compassions fail not. They are new every morning: great is thy faithfulness. The Lord is my portion, saith my soul; therefore will I hope in him.

Lamentations 3:22–24

God's compassion does not fail. Each morning we remember his faithfulness. He is our portion, all that we need. This is comforting. But it means more because it requires God's mercy. Our sins are great, but his mercy is greater. This is how we know the rest of it is true. By his mercy we are not consumed, as we well could be. God is merciful. This is his character and the source of our hope. Every. Single. Day.

*But Christ as a son over
his own house; whose house are we,
if we hold fast the confidence
and the rejoicing of the hope firm
unto the end.*

Hebrews 3:6

*For this God is our God
for ever and ever: he will be our
guide even unto death.*

Psalm 48:14

According to my earnest expectation and my hope, that in nothing I shall be ashamed, but that with all boldness, as always, so now also Christ shall be magnified in my body, whether it be by life, or by death.

Philippians 1:20

The thing I love most about having hope is the promise of that hope being realized one day. God promises me that my hopeful expectations will be fulfilled if I stay on his path, and follow his will. I have no reason to be afraid, feel guilty, or be ashamed when I have hope, because God sees my heart and comes through . . . always. Thank you, God, for never giving me false hope. Thank you for never breaking your promise of reward, either in this life or the next. May my whole life be a testament of the power of hope to others, God, encouraging them to walk with joyful expectation.

When trouble strikes, O God, we are restored by small signs of hope found in ordinary places: friends, random kindness, shared pain and support. Help us collect them like mustard seeds that can grow into a spreading harvest of well-being.

Bow down thine ear, O Lord, hear me:
for I am poor and needy. Preserve my
soul; for I am holy: O thou my God,
save thy servant that trusteth in thee.
Be merciful unto me, O Lord: for I
cry unto thee daily. Rejoice the soul
of thy servant: for unto thee, O Lord,
do I lift up my soul. For thou, Lord,
art good, and ready to forgive; and
plenteous in mercy unto all them that
call upon thee. Give ear, O Lord, unto
my prayer; and attend to the voice of
my supplications. In the day of my
trouble I will call upon thee: for thou
wilt answer me.

Psalm 86:1–7

And we desire that every one of you do shew the same diligence to the full assurance of hope unto the end: That ye be not slothful, but followers of them who through faith and patience inherit the promises.

Hebrews 6:11–12

The book of Hebrews talks a lot about men and women of faith, beginning with Abraham and including an extensive list in chapter 11. Gideon and Samuel, Sara and Joseph: They are all there. The author wants us to be like them, diligent and patient believers who trust God's promises. Be filled with hope to the end, he says. And see them all come true.

In the day of prosperity be joyful, but in the day of adversity consider: God also hath set the one over against the other, to the end that man should find nothing after him.

Ecclesiastes 7:14

They shall not hunger nor thirst;
neither shall the heat nor sun smite them:
for he that hath mercy on them
shall lead them, even by the springs of
water shall he guide them.

Isaiah 49:10

Dear Lord,

I am feeling more hopeful these days. For a while, I forgot to include your loving guidance and grace in my life. I forgot that if I pray and meditate and just get silent enough to listen, you always give me the answers I seek, and the direction I need to overcome anything life hands me. I pray for continued guidance and wisdom, and that I may always live from a place of hope instead of fear, and a place of possibilities instead of limitations. You are my wings and my rock, allowing me to both soar higher and stay grounded. No matter what I may be facing, staying in the comforting light of your presence gives me the hope I need to carry on with my head held high and my heart strong and fearless. Thank you for the gift of hope. Amen.

For we through the Spirit wait for the hope of righteousness by faith.

Galatians 5:5

Without rhyme or reason, hope allays the soul's worries with the certainty of geese who know precisely the day to fly south.

Then they cry unto the Lord in their trouble, and he saveth them out of their distresses. He sent his word, and healed them, and delivered them from their destruction.

Psalm 107:19–20

Thou art my hiding place; thou shalt preserve me from trouble; thou shalt compass me about with songs of deliverance.

Psalm 32:7

Lord, I need a place to hide. I'm overwhelmed, with many things to do and many places to be. Competing demands, some of which I've put on myself, pull at me. Help me, Lord. Give me the wisdom to make good choices. Help me say the right things. Give me a safe and quiet place to hide. Give me a moment of peace and I will sing your praises. Give me a new song, a song of hope and deliverance.

I falter where I firmly trod,
And falling with my weight of cares
Upon the great world's altar stairs
That slope through darkness up to God,
I stretch lame hands of faith, and grope,
And gather dust and chaff, and call
To what I feel is Lord of all,
And faintly trust the larger hope.

—Alfred, Lord Tennyson

Heavenly Father, your grace can refresh
and renew us with the living water of
hope and faith. Please help us fully live
the lives you have given us. Amen.

In that day sing ye unto her,
A vineyard of red wine. I the Lord
do keep it; I will water it every
moment: lest any hurt it, I will keep
it night and day.

Isaiah 27:2–3

Things are about to get rough. Israel will be exiled and Jerusalem will be destroyed. But Israel is God's people and Jerusalem is his city. It will flourish again, as will his vineyard. He will keep it and water it. His people's sorrow will be turned into a song.

Surely God remembers his promises and guards his people. They have been unfaithful and they will suffer the consequences. But in the midst of great devastation, "Israel shall blossom and bud, and fill the face of the world with fruit" (verse 6). He will not forget them. And he will not forget us either.

When we grow discouraged, God, direct our eyes toward spiderwebs spun in a corner and remind us that no hope is too small. At first glance, the webs look like fragile, insignificant strands, but in fact they have amazing strength. And consider what those webs do for the spiders. The webs bring the spiders sustenance. Help us to twist our own tiny strands of hope into sturdy ropes of commitments when we take the next step toward the tasks you are calling us to. Amen.

Every valley shall be filled, and every mountain and hill shall be brought low; and the crooked shall be made straight, and the rough ways shall be made smooth. And all flesh shall see the salvation of God.

Luke 3:5–6

Father, hold us in your arms in the midst of devastation and ruin. Remind us that rampaging nature and human evil will not touch us in our eternal homes. Send your angels to remind us that our lives and homes on earth are part of the journey, not our final destination. Amen.

Behold, the days come, saith the Lord, that I will perform that good thing which I have promised unto the house of Israel and to the house of Judah.

Jeremiah 33:14

God will perform the good thing he has promised. We see it in the story of his people. Sometimes he promises them blessing; sometimes he promises them judgment. He always keeps his promise. The good thing in view here is restoration after exile and captivity. And a Savior. That's a good thing for all of us. That's a promise we can depend on.

Almighty God, sometimes the floods of life leave us devastated and defeated. Our tears flow like rivers pushing over their banks. In our worst moments, you give us comfort and hope. Amen.

*But I trust in the Lord Jesus to
send Timotheus shortly unto you,
that I also may be of good comfort,
when I know your state.*

Philippians 2:19

Creator God, you have come to me with
healing in your hand. When I cried
out, you heard me. You provided me
with a gift that brought both peace and
pleasure to my harried life. You helped
me to focus on life instead of illness
and sorrow. Lord, thank you for this
wondrous gift. Amen.

Grace of my heart, I turn to you when I am feeling lost and alone. You restore me with strength and hope and the courage to face a new day. You bless me with joy and comfort me through trials and tribulations. You direct my thoughts, guide my actions, and temper my words. You give me the patience and kindness I need to be good. Grace of my heart, I turn to you. Amen.

For whatsoever things were written aforetime were written for our learning, that we through patience and comfort of the scriptures might have hope.

Romans 15:4

While all the Bible was written for us, not all of it was written to us. Some of the promises were written for certain individuals or for certain situations. Context is important in understanding who was promised what. But all of the promises are written so that through "patience and comfort" we "might have hope." This in itself is a wonderful promise. The promises of God tell us something about God. We learn about his character and power by the things he says and does. Whatever he promises or does tells us something about who he is and what he wants. It is in him, after all, that all the treasures of wisdom are hidden—and found.

*Also I heard the voice of the Lord,
saying, Whom shall I send,
and who will go for us? Then said I,
Here am I; send me.*

Isaiah 6:8

*Fear none of those things
which thou shalt suffer...Be thou
faithful unto death, and I
will give thee a crown of life.*

Revelation 2:10

Unlike the more complacent church
at Ephesus, the church at Smyrna had
already begun to suffer for its faith. This
is the second letter written by John for
Jesus to churches during the end of the
first century. He tells the congregation
that those who overcome will "not be hurt
of the second death" (verse 11). Believers
were burned and tossed to wild animals
in the coliseums. But they would only die
once. Their persecutors would die and
then, after the judgments, die again. Not
only would the believers not be hurt by
the second death, they would receive a
crown of life. Their reward would be an
eternal one, their trial a short one.

Have not I commanded thee?
Be strong and of a good courage;
be not afraid, neither be thou
dismayed: for the Lord thy God is
with thee whithersoever thou goest.

Joshua 1:9

Security, loving God, is going to sleep in the assurance that you know our hearts before we speak and are waiting, as soon as you hear from us, to transform our concerns into hope and action, our loneliness into companionship, and our despair into dance.

When the storms of life surround us,
Lord, we cannot see the light of the sun
behind the clouds, and so we forget it is
there. The winds blow hard upon us, and
the cold air chills us, but once the storm
has passed, we stand in the sun again,
and we find we have been cleansed.

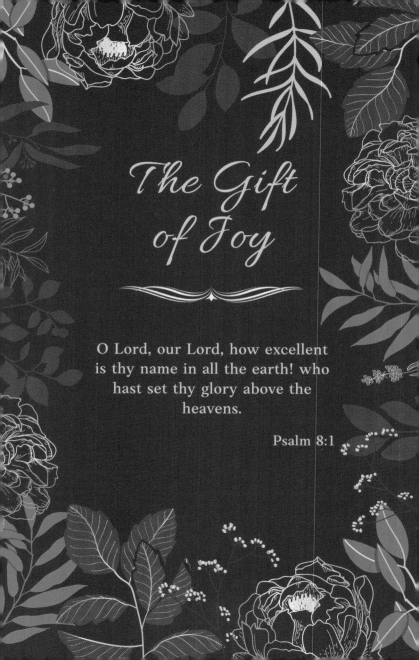

The Gift of Joy

O Lord, our Lord, how excellent
is thy name in all the earth! who
hast set thy glory above the
heavens.

Psalm 8:1

O God, who by the grace of the Holy Ghost hast poured the gifts of love into the hearts of thy faithful people, grant unto all thy servants in thy mercy health of body and soul, that they may love thee with all their strength, and with perfect affection fulfill thy pleasure; through Jesus Christ our Lord. Amen.

6th-century prayer

Let your light so shine before men, that they may see your good works, and glorify your Father which is in heaven.

Matthew 5:16

God, Creator of all things, ultimately all light comes from you. I praise you and glorify you, Father God, source and giver of all good things.

Now thank we all our God
with hearts and hands and voices,
who wondrous things hath done,
in whom this world rejoices;
who, from our mothers' arms,
hath blessed us on our way
with countless gifts of love,
and still is ours today.

—Martin Rinkart,
translated by Catherine Winkworth

Not for that we have dominion over your faith, but are helpers of your joy: for by faith ye stand.

2 Corinthians 1:24

My mother was a joyful person. She faced challenges like everyone else—her health in particular troubled her off and on through most of her adult life—but as a rule, she chose to focus on the positive. Her joyful outlook took many forms—she was a calm, good listener; she embraced new experiences; she was interested and interesting. And something that strikes me now is how her radiant spirit was often contagious. I myself would sometimes return from school glum or discouraged, but if we spent some quiet time together—working in the garden, say, or sometimes I would finish my homework in the kitchen while Mom cooked dinner—my own spirits lifted. Mom died last year, and as an adult, I am left to carry her bright torch for my own family. God, help me to always remember how important it is to share our joy with others so that they may experience it.

Also that day they offered great sacrifices, and rejoiced: for God had made them rejoice with great joy: the wives also and the children rejoiced: so that the joy of Jerusalem was heard even afar off.

Nehemiah 12:43

Amazing grace!
How sweet the sound
That saved a wretch like me;
I once was lost, but now I'm found;
Was blind, but now I see.
'Twas grace that taught my heart to fear,
And grace my fears relieved;
How precious did that grace appear
The hour I first believed.
Through many dangers, toils and snares
I have already come,
'Tis grace that brought me safe thus far,
And grace will lead me home.

—John Newton

Turn again our captivity, O Lord, as the streams in the south. They that sow in tears shall reap in joy. He that goeth forth and weepeth, bearing precious seed, shall doubtless come again with rejoicing, bringing his sheaves with him.

Psalm 126:4–6

And it shall come to pass, that whosoever shall call on the name of the Lord shall be saved.

Acts 2:21

God promises we will have a joyous, prosperous life if we do nothing more than call upon him. That's it! We don't have to suffer for his love and miracles. We just have to be willing to invite his presence into our hearts and our homes and we can be transformed. This is such a powerful and profound truth, and yet how many times do we try to live our own will and force life to be what we think it should be? How often does that work out? God, I pray you will always be the biggest part of my life, and that your presence will always guide me. I pray that the bond we share grows stronger with time and that my faith and trust in you will be rewarded.

Ye also, as lively stones, are built up a spiritual house, an holy priesthood, to offer up spiritual sacrifices, acceptable to God by Jesus Christ.

1 Peter 2:5

When I read this passage, I think of beautiful polished gemstones and colorful mosaics. You can build us into something truly beautiful! God, it is your love that flows through us, so that we are able to love you and our neighbors. Thank you for making us beautiful to your eyes.

For the beauty of the earth,
For the glory of the skies;
For the love which from our birth,
Over and around us lies;
Lord of all, to Thee we raise
This, our hymn of grateful praise.
For the joy of human love,
Brother, sister, parent, child;
Friends on Earth and friends above,
For all gentle thoughts and mild;
Lord of all, to Thee we raise
This, our hymn of grateful praise.

—Folliott S. Pierpoint

God, I ask in prayer that you help me hold the vision of a better world, and that I may clearly know my role in making that better world a reality. Let my vision join that of others, to create a more joyful world for those who come after us. Amen.

And ye now therefore have sorrow:
but I will see you again, and
your heart shall rejoice, and your
joy no man taketh from you.

John 16:22

Jesus concludes his last discourse by
reminding his disciples he will be leaving
them. He has comforted them and prepared
them: He will prepare them a place, he will
answer their prayers, and he will give them
fruit. But the greatest comfort of all is this: "I
will see you again."

The real joy is not in the things he does or
we do. The real joy is his presence. When
he returns, we will see him and be glad.
Through sorrow and difficulty, the apostles,
the early church, and believers today have
longed for him to return and be with us. His
presence is a true comfort and joy; no one
can take it away.

Rejoice, and be exceeding glad: for great is your reward in heaven: for so persecuted they the prophets which were before you.

Matthew 5:12

When my courage wavers, when it would be difficult to witness to my faith, let me be inspired by the faith of those who came before me. Hold me fast to my convictions, God, so I may honor you and not stray from your path.

The stone which the builders refused is become the headstone of the corner. This is the Lord's doing; it is marvelous in our eyes.

Psalm 118:22–23

How wonderful when God shows us the beauty in something we thought was worthless! I am grateful for the times God opened my eyes to unexpected beauty. Help me to keep my mind open to the wonders all around me and to appreciate everything I see, no matter how insignificant it may seem.

Young children have a particularly deep capacity for joy. They love fiercely and play hard; their worldview is often one of opportunity and abundance. As we grow, experiences good and bad accrue. We take on more responsibility, for others and for ourselves, and can lose sight of that deep well of joy. It's still there, if we are mindful. But joy is tricky in that it can manifest itself in opposites: There is joy in community, even as it exists in solitary pursuits. A gorgeous summer sky brings joy, as does a brooding landscape. Sometimes we don't recognize joy, but it is there: We can still access it, whether it feels like good loneliness, hilarity, or a deep stillness. It is a gift we must not lose sight of. Dear Lord, thank you for joy, which comes from you.

These things have I spoken unto you, that my joy might remain in you, and that your joy might be full.

John 15:11

For nature around me, I thank you.

For grass and tree, I thank you.

For sun and rain, I thank you.

For fields of grain, I thank you.

For cloudy skies, I thank you.

For mountain highs, I thank you.

For desert flowers, I thank you.

For twilight hours, I thank you.

A merry heart doeth good like a medicine: but a broken spirit drieth the bones.

Proverbs 17:22

Last summer I started bicycling regularly for my health. One day late in August I jumped a curb too exuberantly, wiped out, and broke my leg. Fortunately, I work from home, so my schedule was not too affected during my recuperation time. And yet, because I am by nature an active person, the limitations of my injury—not to mention the bulky cast—put a real cramp in my style. I'll confess that some days I felt down. My good friends Dave and Sara were a lifeline during this time. They'd stop by to watch movies, bring in dinner, or just "hang out." We laughed a lot during these visits and I invariably found that after they looked in on me, my mood soared and I felt better overall. Long after my leg has healed, I remember their kindness with gratitude. Lord, thank you for the friends and loved ones who uplift me. Just as exercise, being joyful is good for my health!

Today I am going to treat myself! Thank you for the opportunity to do something special "just because." Thank you for giving me the chance to reward myself just for being me.

I am grateful for these little joys and for the ability to recognize that I am worthy of pampering. My life is special, and today I am thankful for the chance to rejoice in myself.

There is that speaketh like the piercings of a sword: but the tongue of the wise is health.

Proverbs 12:18

Few things are as healing as a good word or the right word at the right moment. It can heal our spirits, encouraging and strengthening us better than any tonic. "Heaviness in the heart of man maketh it stoop: but a good word maketh it glad." (verse 25). A cheerful word, in fact, "doeth good like a medicine" (Proverbs 17:22).

Our gracious words can chase the shadows from a friend's face and give them "a cheerful countenance" (Proverbs 15:13) that reflects confidence and hope. Better yet, this gladness of heart reduces the anxiety and stress that eats away at them and affects their physical health. No wonder a cheerful word does good, like medicine.

Thank you, Lord, for the inner light that shines within me. Help me to show that light to others and not hide it deep inside myself. Thank you for my talents and the things that I am good at. May I never forget how grateful I am to be able to share my abilities and bring joy to others.

O let the nations be glad and sing for joy: for thou shalt judge the people righteously, and govern the nations upon earth.

Psalm 67:4

Heavenly Father, when I stop for a moment and just think about all the blessings you've showered on me, I'm filled with joy and happiness. I often complain about my problems and focus on the things I wish I had, but in these quiet moments I truly become aware of just how few problems I do have and how much you've given me. Thank you for slowing down my often hectic and crazy life every now and then so I can recognize these moments of pure joy.

A happy attitude is food for the spirit. Staying in God's grace makes the challenges of life a little easier. Lessons are learned with less effort. Mercy is given more freely. Joy returns!

Today I take joy in nature. I look around and see all that you have made. The natural world is full of your presence. Thank you for the birds migrating overhead, for the wind's breath, even for the violence of a thunderstorm. I know that everything came to be by your hand, and the world around me is a blessing in my life.

God, help me notice the little things and be grateful for them. All too often, we rush through life and don't notice the blessings all around us. I am grateful for the chance to see beauty in the smallest details. Help me remember to slow down and look. I am grateful for the little bits of beauty scattered through my day.

Jesus, every time I stop to think of it, I am awed that you provided salvation for us at the price of your own life. Thank you for opening up the way for me to enjoy eternal life with you. May my being be filled with joy, gratitude, and awe at every mention of your name.

The king shall joy in thy strength,
O Lord; and in thy salvation
how greatly shall he rejoice!

Psalm 21:1

Sometimes a stranger smiles at me in passing,
and it is a beautiful, joy-filled, light-giving
smile. It makes me want to know their secret
to happiness! I think their secret is probably
you, O Lord. Please let me be so happy in
your presence that I radiate your warmth and
love even to those who are strangers.

A new heart also will I give you, and a new spirit will I put within you: and I will take away the stony heart out of your flesh, and I will give you a heart of flesh.

Ezekiel 36:26

Lord, I open my eyes and all I see are the amazing blessings that surround me. In this moment, I want for nothing, and I live with the knowledge that I can always turn to you for help, and cast my cares upon you, when my clarity and my vision cloud with worry. Thank you, Lord, for reminding me that the joyful blessings of this moment are all because of your love for me.

But none of these things move me,
neither count I my life dear
unto myself, so that I might finish
my course with joy, and the ministry,
which I have received of the
Lord Jesus, to testify the gospel
of the grace of God.

Acts 20:24

We are products of our environment. I
learned from my parents, who learned
from their parents, and it is not just what
children hear—it is what they see, day in
and day out. My parents were good people.
They are both deceased, but I believe
they are in heaven. I also believe it is my
responsibility to live in such a way that
carries on their legacy of dignity and grace.
I can model that behavior for my own
children, teens now, and in so doing inspire
them to choose a life informed by Christ's
teachings. It is an awesome responsibility
to live in such a way that others are
inspired to seek the joy of heaven.

And now, little children, abide in him; that, when he shall appear, we may have confidence, and not be ashamed before him at his coming.

1 John 2:28

Our joy at his coming will not be because we tried harder but because we are abiding in him. The word abide means to dwell in or to be at home with. We abide in him by living in his grace. Abiding is that important and it is that easy.

*Blessed is the people that know the
joyful sound: they shall walk, O Lord,
in the light of thy countenance.*

Psalm 89:15

Lord, there's that joy-filled song "Walkin'
on Sunshine" that comes to mind when I
read this verse. And for me, the happiness
of being in the light with you, the delight of
walking with you, and the ongoing fellowship
with my brothers and sisters in you—all this
knowing that you've washed my sins away—
walkin' on sunshine is just what it feels like.
Thank you for calling me into your light!

May you learn to let your happiness depend, day by day, not upon something you could possibly lose, but upon that which could never, ever pass away.

Rejoice in the Lord always: and again I say, Rejoice. Let your moderation be known unto all men. The Lord is at hand. Be careful for nothing; but in every thing by prayer and supplication with thanksgiving let your requests be made known unto God.

Philippians 4:4–6

Lord, we praise you for all the beauty and wonder you've placed in the world. How creative of you to think of a creature as exuberant and joyful as the hummingbird! How interesting that you sprinkled spots on the backs of the newborn fawns that follow along behind their mother through our backyard. Let us never become so accustomed to your glorious creation that we take it for granted, Lord. You've blessed us with a wonderland, and we thank you for it.

For verily I say unto you, That whosoever shall say unto this mountain, Be thou removed, and be thou cast into the sea; and shall not doubt in his heart, but shall believe that those things which he saith shall come to pass; he shall have whatsoever he saith.

Mark 11:23

Heavenly Father, what can be more joyful than to realize that through you, all things are possible? Even when I'm at the lowest point in my life, I only have to reach out to you, and you take me and lift me up again. Though there is much trouble and hardship in my life right now, my joy is knowing that you have reserved a place for me in your heavenly kingdom. Thank you, Father.

Dear God, what joy we have in gathering to pray and praise you together. How encouraging it is to share what's happening on our separate life journeys and see your hand at work in so many different ways. Thank you for arranging those times of fellowship, Lord. They are blessed times indeed.

Immanuel—what a beautiful word! It means "God with us." The reality of the birth of Jesus is that he is God, come to be with us, wrapped up in human likeness, and ultimately placed upon a cross as the greatest gift ever given. Now, since his resurrection and ascension, his Spirit remains with us, and we are never alone. Immanuel—God is with us at this very moment.

O God, thou art life, wisdom, truth, bounty, and blessedness, the eternal, the only true good! My God and my Lord, thou art my hope and my heart's joy. I confess, with thanksgiving, that thou hast made me in thine image, that I may direct all my thoughts to thee, and love thee. Lord, make me to know thee aright, that I may more and more love, and enjoy, and possess thee. And since, in the life here below, I cannot fully attain this blessedness, let it at least grow in me day by day, until it all be fulfilled at last in the life to come. Here be the knowledge of thee increased, and there let it be perfected. Here let my love to thee grow, and there let it ripen; that my joy being here great in hope, may there in fruition be made perfect. Amen.

—St. Anselm

Let the word of Christ dwell in you richly in all wisdom; teaching and admonishing one another in psalms and hymns and spiritual songs, singing with grace in your hearts to the Lord.

Colossians 3:16

Will tomorrow be less hectic and more inclined toward joy? Will I be less tired? God help me, I'm not waiting to find out. In your creation, joy can be found anytime, but mostly now. Keep reminding me that now is all of life I can hold at any moment. It cannot be banked, invested, hoarded, or saved. It can only be spent.

*But the fruit of the Spirit is
love, joy, peace, longsuffering,
gentleness, goodness, faith,
meekness, temperance:
against such there is no law.*

Galatians 5:22–23

It is easy to tell if the Spirit of God is
active in our life. All anyone has to do it
look at the fruit. Is your life characterized
by love, joy, peace? Are you known for
your patience, gentleness, and moderation?
If not, ask God to make you more fruitful
today, filling you with his Spirit. Others
will see and be glad.